Make the *in GCSE*

Computer
Studies

James Gatenby

TEACH YOURSELF BOOKS
Hodder and Stoughton

First published 1989

Copyright © 1989
James Gatenby

No part of this publication may be reproduced
or transmitted in any form or by any means,
electronically or mechanically, including
photocopying, recording or any information
storage or retrieval system, without either
the prior permission in writing from the publisher
or a licence, permitting restricted copying,
issued by the Copyright Licensing Agency,
33–34 Alfred Place, London WC1E 7DP

British Library Cataloguing in Publication Data
Gatenby, James
Make the grade in GCSE computer studies.—
(Teach yourself books).
1. Computer sciences
I. Title
004

ISBN 0 340 50057 3

Printed in Great Britain for
Hodder and Stoughton Educational,
a division of Hodder and Stoughton Ltd,
Mill Road, Dunton Green, Sevenoaks, Kent,
by Richard Clay Ltd, Bungay, Suffolk
Photoset by Rowland Phototypesetting Ltd,
Bury St Edmunds, Suffolk

CONTENTS

ACKNOWLEDGEMENTS

The following examining groups have given permission for their examination questions to be used:

London and East Anglian Group (LEAG)
Southern Examining Group (SEG)
Midland Examining Group (MEG)
Northern Examining Association (NEA)
Welsh Joint Education Committee (WJEC)
Northern Ireland Schools Examinations Council (NISEC)
Scottish Examinations Board (SEB)

The author and publishers would like to thank the following for their help and permission to reproduce copyright material:

Psion Ltd
Austin Rover Group Ltd
Digital Research Ltd
National Girobank
National Westminster Bank PLC
Apple Computer UK Ltd
Hewlett-Packard Ltd
Denford Machine Tools Ltd
British Telecommunications PLC (Prestel)
Bank of Scotland
Ferranti Computer Systems Ltd
The Ford Motor Company Ltd
Acorn Computers Ltd
Research Machines Ltd
IBM United Kingdom Ltd

INTRODUCTION

The GCSE courses in Computing and Information Technology are popular options for students. This is not surprising, for computing can be exciting and enjoyable. At the same time, the new technology is so important in the modern world that all school and college students should have experience of it. GCSE places less emphasis on the component parts of computers than did the previous GCE/CSE Computer Studies syllabuses; although it is still necessary to understand the basic principles of computers it is now the *applications* of information technology which are considered most important. This reflects the changing role of the computer from its previous narrow function as a 'number crunching' machine used in maths and science. Now computers are smaller, more powerful and more *versatile* – their applications include art, design, music and publishing as well as traditional data processing involving text and numbers.

The GCSE courses encourage students to demonstrate *positive achievement* over an extended period – nearly two years – and much of this includes continually-assessed coursework. In GCSE, students follow a syllabus provided by one of the six regional examination boards; all students generally attempt the same work over the two years of the course. In the final examination, students receive a grade from A to G. Two basic arrangements exist to provide for the different levels of attainment of students:

Either:

1   All students attempt the same questions, which are designed to allow candidates to demonstrate their differing abilities. These may include 'open-ended' questions such as 'Discuss the main concerns arising from the storage of personal data on computers . . .'

or:

2   Students are entered for *different papers* at either higher or lower levels. Entries are made around Christmas in the final year and should be based on a review of the student's work and discussion between the teacher and student. There may be further opportunity to discuss the entry at a parents' evening. One effect of these *differentiated* papers is that, for example, a student sitting papers at the lower level in some examinations may be excluded from the possibility of grades A and B.

The exact details for each course vary, but as a rough guide the content of the course will be as follows:

Written Papers	50% approx.
Written Paper (Case Study)	15–30% approx.
Project Work	25–40% approx.

Exact details of the syllabus followed by your particular school or college may be obtained from the appropriate examination board. (Please see the list of names and addresses at the end of this section.) In addition, all the specialist computer 'jargon' used in textbooks and examination papers is defined in the booklet *Glossary of Computing Terms – An Introduction* published by the Cambridge University Press for the British Computer Society. This may be obtained from bookshops.

Examination papers
This book has been written after a thorough review of the examination papers from the various examination boards. These must all satisfy a common core content laid down by the National Criteria for Computer Studies.

Multiple choice questions (or objective tests)
Some of the boards offer questions which require a single answer to be chosen from four or five given answers – usually by ringing the correct answer or marking a special answer sheet for input to a computer. Sometimes one of the answers is ridiculous, and may be discounted. A typical multiple choice question might be:

Which of the following is not a computer input device?
A Keyboard
B Joystick
C Graph plotter
D Mouse

Always make sure your answer is clear; if you have second thoughts about a particular answer there will be a definite method of changing it. If necessary guess at an answer rather than leaving it blank.

Longer questions
Most examinations contain some questions of a more open-ended nature such as: 'Discuss the effects of computers on employment . . .'. These questions may be answered in the form of an essay but this should be kept brief and to the point. Don't waffle or use flowery language – the examiner will be looking for certain key facts so an orderly list may be quite adequate. Many candidates lose marks because, although they may write long and technically correct statements of fact, they do not answer the specific question set. In a long question this could be disastrous.

READ THE QUESTIONS CAREFULLY

The Case Study Paper (or Applications Study)
This paper will examine your knowledge of a prescribed topic. Your teacher will provide detailed notes and there may be computer software to simulate the process in school or college. The case study will be based around the use of computers in a real-life data processing operation such as a large library or supermarket.

Apart from the written examination paper based on the case study, the content of the case study will provide much useful information. This should be relevant in the other written examination papers and may also be helpful in your project work. For example, the study of the *security* of data files in a supermarket may provide useful background research material for part of a project involving data files.

Project work

The three main components of the course – written theory papers, written case study paper, and coursework projects – should not be seen in isolation, in separate compartments; they should complement and 'feed' off each other. One of the main aims of GCSE is that students learn while carrying out active project work, rather than always copying notes from the blackboard or a book (although this is still needed sometimes).

So a well-chosen project will not only provide interest and enjoyment but should also help you to learn much of the *theoretical* work needed for the examinations. For example, a project involving a database should include important topics such as the design of a system, the collection and preparation of the data, checking the data for errors (verification and validation), processing the data in the computer and checking the output for accuracy. Project work should also include consideration of the security and privacy of the data. A final report must be written giving a critical analysis of the whole system with its merits, disadvantages and possible alternative solutions. Of course, the work you do using the computer is only a part of the project – there should also be research from books and magazines, etc.

As an example, the writing of an arcade-style computer game might be very stimulating and require a lot of serious problem solving. However, this sort of project may not fulfil the important role of active learning about the broader aspects of computing. Although it would certainly demonstrate a knowledge of programming, a computer games project would probably need to be 'topped up' by a second project which filled in some of the gaps in the coursework requirements. Coursework projects should *complement* each other in covering the syllabus.

A sensible timetable for coursework
Project work should be started early in the first year of the course and written up *continuously*; without evidence that you will complete satisfactory final projects, your teacher may not enter you for the examination. Aim to have all coursework projects written up by Christmas of the final year. This prevents a last-minute rush to use crowded computing facilities such as printers. The final year is really only about nine months and this time goes extremely quickly. Time will be lost for trial or 'mock' examinations, holidays and possibly work experience.

Further notes on coursework are given in the Appendix in this book.

Revision
This should be started before the trial examinations, which ought to be a complete 'dress-rehearsal' of the final examination. The trial or 'mock' examinations should be taken seriously; your attainment in this examination may decide the level of your entry in the final examination and therefore the range of grades possible.

A major part of your revision should include systematically working through *past papers*; this book contains sample questions in each chapter and your teacher should provide complete papers. Sets of past papers can be obtained from bookshops or directly from the examination boards. In the early stages, it may be necessary to make frequent reference to textbooks for the answers to some questions. Later, you should attempt the papers in strict examination conditions. Your teacher may set up some more practice examinations; if not, perhaps you have a quiet area at home or school where this is possible. Precise timing of these 'examinations' is important.

Apart from books like this one, which should be helpful for revision and for reference throughout the course, keep a close watch on the news media – television, radio and newspapers. These often carry relevant items on new applications of computers or social implications such as jobs lost or created.

The day of the examination
Once in the examination room, listen carefully to the invigilator; there may be important changes to the paper notified at the last minute. Finally, read the instructions thoroughly so that you are quite sure which parts of the examination to attempt. If in doubt, ask the invigilator before the examination gets under way. Work steadily through the questions. Don't spend too long thinking about a difficult question – carry on to the next one and go back to the unfinished questions later.

Addresses of the GCSE examination boards

LONDON & EAST ANGLIAN GROUP (LEAG)

EAEB
East Anglian Examinations Board,
The Lindens,
Lexden Road,
Colchester,
Essex. CO3 3RL

LREB
London Regional Examining Board,
Lyon House,
104 Wandsworth High St,
London. SW18 4LF

London
University of London Schools Examinations Board,
Stewart House,
32 Russell Square,
London. WC1B 5DP

SOUTHERN EXAMINING GROUP (SEG)

SREB
Southern Regional Examinations Board,
Avondale House,
33 Carlton Crescent,
Southampton. SO9 4YL

SEREB
South East Regional Examinations Board,
Beloe House,
2–10 Mount Ephraim Road,
Tunbridge Wells. TN1 1EU

AEB
The Associated Examining Board,
Stag Hill House,
Guildford,
Surrey. GU2 5XJ

SWEB
South Western Examinations Board,
23–29 Marsh Street,
Bristol. BS1 4BP

Oxford
University of Oxford Delegacy of Local Examinations,
Ewert Place,
Summertown,
Oxford. OX7 7BZ

MIDLAND EXAMINING GROUP (MEG)

EMREB
East Midlands Regional Examinations Board,
Robins Wood House,
Robins Wood Road,
Aspley,
Nottingham. NG8 3NR

Cambridge
University of Cambridge Local Examinations Syndicate,
Syndicate Buildings,
1 Hills Road,
Cambridge. CB1 2EU

WMEB
West Midlands Examinations Board,
Norfolk House,
Smallbrook,
Queensway,
Birmingham. B5 4NJ

SUJB
Southern Universities' Joint Board for School Examinations,
Cotham Road,
Bristol. BS6 6DD

O & C
Oxford & Cambridge Schools Examinations Board,
10 Trumpington Street,
Cambridge. CB2 1QB

NORTHERN EXAMINING ASSOCIATION (NEA)

JMB
Joint Matriculation Board,
Devas Street,
Manchester. M15 6EU

ALSEB
Associated Lancashire Schools Examining Board,
12 Harter Street,
Manchester. M1 6HL

NWREB
North West Regional Examinations Board,
Orbit House, Albert Street, Eccles,
Manchester. M30 0WL

YHREB
Yorkshire & Humberside Regional Examinations Board
31–33 Springfield Avenue,
Harrogate,
North Yorkshire. HG1 2HW

Sheffield Office
Scarsdale House,
136 Derbyshire Lane,
Sheffield. S8 8SE

NREB
North Regional Examinations Board,
Wheatfield Road,
Westerhope,
Newcastle upon Tyne. NE5 5JZ

WALES

WJEC
Welsh Joint Education Committee
245 Western Avenue,
Cardiff. CF5 2YX

SCOTLAND

SEB
Scottish Examination Board,
Ironmills Road,
Dalkeith,
Midlothian. EH22 1LE

NORTHERN IRELAND

NISEC
Northern Ireland Schools Examinations Council,
Beechill House,
42 Beechill Road,
Belfast. BT8 4RS

Computer systems exist in three main categories according to physical size. These are, in descending order of size,

mainframe
minicomputer
microcomputer

Mainframe
This is a large computer consisting of many different cabinets. It requires a spacious room or suite of rooms. The mainframe can cost millions of pounds and is used by large organisations such as governments, armed forces, local authorities, banks and industrial corporations. The mainframe computer will support a large number (over 100) of *terminals* (keyboards + screens). IBM is the dominant manufacturer of mainframe computers.

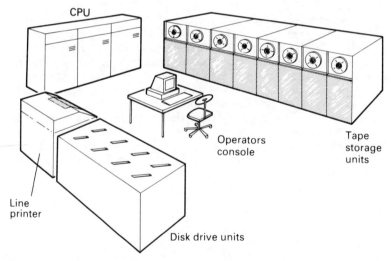

Fig. 1.1 *Mainframe computer*

Minicomputer
This consists of a few cabinets capable of fitting into a small room. The minicomputer can support several terminals and costs in the range of £5000–£100 000. Minicomputers are used by colleges, small businesses or branch offices of large organisations. The *VAX* minicomputer made by DEC is well established, together with machines from IBM.

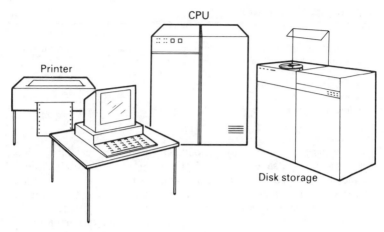

Fig. 1.2 *Minicomputer*

Microcomputer – desktop

These often rival minicomputers in performance (speed and storage capacity). Their small size was made possible by the development of the *silicon chip/microprocessor*. Microcomputers may be used as independent, *stand-alone* devices or as terminals to mini or mainframe computers. A small *home micro* can be bought for less than £100 while more powerful *business/scientific* machines cost several thousand pounds. The business micro world is dominated by machines from IBM, which has set the industry standard; there are many cheaper copies of this standard, known as *clones*, or *IBM compatibles*. Amongst the most successful of these is the Amstrad PC range. A business micro is generally known as a *PC* (*Personal Computer*).

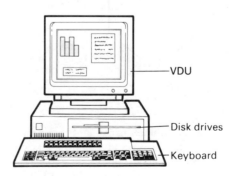

Fig. 1.3 *Desktop microcomputer*

Microcomputer – portable or 'laptop'

Apart from the normal desktop micro, there are various *portable* machines which until recently were referred to as 'luggables' because of their weight. Lightweight *battery-powered* machines such as the Cambridge Computers Z88 are genuinely portable and are suitable for use in many situations away from the office. These might include typing notes in a conference or making calculations while travelling on a train. Although these machines can use quite powerful business *software* (e.g. *wordprocessor*, *spreadsheet*, *database*) they are small and quiet and do not disturb other people nearby.

Large *files* of data can be saved in the computer's memory (which is battery-powered). These files can be transferred to a larger office machine (e.g. IBM or compatible) when the user returns to base. Similarly, a journalist can transmit text to the office by connecting the portable computer to a telephone line using a device known as a *modem*.

Fig. 1.4 *Portable computer*

There are also *hand-held* microcomputers (as opposed to calculators) which are fully programmable and have many of the features of much larger machines. An example is the *Psion Organiser*.

Fig. 1.5 *Hand-held computer*

Relationship between mainframe, mini and micro

A national building society might handle 10 million accounts through several hundred branches in different parts of the country. Head office would have a mainframe computer; each branch would have a mini-computer linked by cable to the central mainframe; connected to the minicomputer might be 7–10 terminals. The terminals are a mixture of microcomputers and *dumb terminals* (keyboard + screen). The microcomputer can be used as a stand-alone device for doing work independent of the mainframe. The dumb terminal has no independent processing power – it is simply an *input/output* device giving access to the mainframe computer.

Early microcomputers of the late 1970s, such as the Commodore Pet, typically had 32 *kilobytes* of memory (1K is 1024 characters). Data was handled in 'chunks' of 8 *bits* (binary digits). Modern micros such as the Apple Macintosh and the IBM PS/2 have several *megabytes* (millions of characters) of memory and handle data in 32-bit chunks or *words*.

Mainframe computers typically used in High Street banks, etc., work with 64-bit words. With 64 megabytes of main memory, disk backing storage is measured in *gigabytes* (1 gigabyte = 1 billion characters).

Units of memory

A character is a letter, digit (0–9), symbol or punctuation mark
A bit is a binary digit, 0 or 1
A byte is 8 bits
A byte can store one character
A word is one or more bytes
1 kilobyte (K) is 1024 bytes
1 megabyte (Mb) is 1024 kilobytes (about 1 million bytes)

There is an overlap between the sort of tasks carried out by the three types of computer, micro, mini and mainframe. However, large tasks such as processing electricity or gas bills would typically be carried out on a mainframe, as would long and complex engineering and scientific calculations, e.g. in designing a new aircraft, or the handling of 13 000 000 customers' accounts for a building society. A minicomputer might be adequate for the accounts and stock control in a medium sized company. A microcomputer would typically be used by a secretary for *wordprocessing* or by a manager making financial predictions using a spreadsheet program. Microcomputers are also used in education – *Computer Aided Learning (CAL)* – and in the home for games or small business activities, personal finance, etc.

Despite the physical differences in the three main types of computer, the basic principles of their operation are the same. *Data* consisting of numbers, words, sound or pictures are entered into the computer's memory; operations are performed on the data, such as *calculation*, *sorting* into order, making alterations, etc. After processing, the results are copied from the memory onto the screen or printed on paper. The processing of data is carried out by a set of *instructions*, stored alongside the data in the computer's memory. The set of instructions is known as a *program*; the concept of a *stored program* is attributed to the American scientist *Von Neumann*.

The three stages of computing
The overall process of using an electronic computer to convert *raw data* into useful *information* can be broken down into three distinct phases:

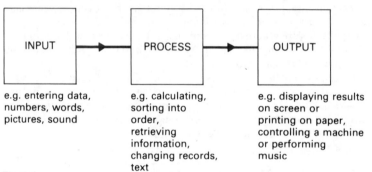

Fig. 1.6

The parts of a computer
The main components of any computer system are:

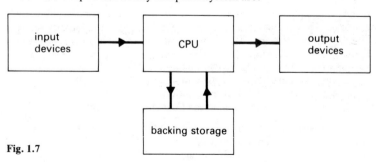

Fig. 1.7

The *Central Processing Unit (CPU)* carries out all of the calculating, etc. The input, output and backing storage units are connected to the CPU and are collectively known as *peripheral units*.

The Central Processing Unit (CPU)

The Central Processing Unit is often referred to as the 'heart' of a computer, since it is the place where much of the work is done. The CPU contains the computer's memory, where both *programs* and *data* are stored. Most computers nowadays are known as *digital devices*; this means that all input, whether it is numbers, letters, pictures or sound, is eventually *coded* into *digits* for processing in the CPU. Other computers work on *physical* measurements such as voltage, but these are used in specialist applications in science, etc. These are known as *analogue* computers and are relatively rare nowadays.

Bits and bytes

It is necessary in digital electronic computers to use the *binary number system* which employs only the digits 0 and 1. This is called a *two-state system*. *Binary digits* are known as *bits*.

Usually bits are grouped in sets of eight – known as *bytes*. Bytes of data are stored in the computer's memory and are also transmitted around the computer, e.g. as output to a printer.

A *picture* would be stored as a set of *x,y coordinates*. The coordinates are converted to bytes and the picture is said to have been *digitised*. A picture can also be stored as a set of minute *pixels* or picture elements on the screen. Bytes in memory would contain the colour and intensity of the pixel.

A typical byte stored in the memory would be:

1	0	1	0	1	0	0	1

Fig. 1.8

Contents of a byte

An important principle of the digital computer is that a byte can be used to represent:

1 *Data*, e.g. the code for a character (a letter of the alphabet or a punctuation mark) or the representation of a decimal number.
2 An *instruction*, e.g. to perform addition.
3 The *address* or position of a piece of data in the memory.

(In practice several bytes may be combined into a *word* to represent an address, a number or an instruction.)

All computer processing operations, even if they involve art, music or the text of a letter, require binary data to be temporarily held in the *Random Access Memory (RAM)*. The memory requires electricity and so all programs and data are lost when the computer is switched off; this temporary memory is said to be *volatile*.

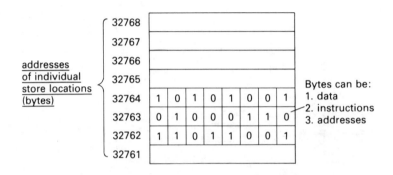

Fig. 1.9 *RAM: Random Access Memory*

The three parts of the CPU
The CPU consists of:

the Immediate Access Store (IAS) (memory)
the Arithmetic and Logic Unit (ALU)
the Control Unit

Most computer processing can be reduced to simple binary arithmetic, such as addition or subtraction. This task is performed by part of the CPU known as the *Arithmetic and Logic Unit (ALU)*. Data stored as bytes in the memory (main store) of the CPU has to be fetched to the ALU when needed and the answers returned to memory afterwards. The flow of data around the system is coordinated by the *Control Unit*; each *store location* in the memory has an *address* (represented by a byte). The Control Unit includes a *program counter* which holds the address of the next instruction to be carried out. The process of reading and carrying out instructions from memory is known as the *fetch–execute* cycle. The Control Unit also supervises the flow of data (as bytes) to the *peripheral units* of the computer, such as the printer, and the storage devices, such as disk drives.

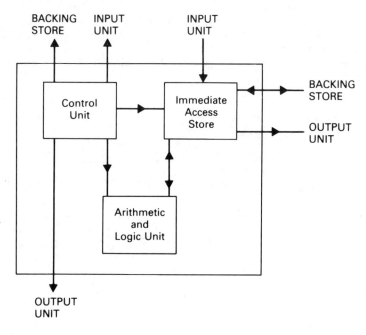

Fig. 1.10   *The Central Processing Unit (CPU)*

Peripheral units
These are devices connected to the Central Processing Unit, and are used for input, permanent (backing) storage, and output of information.

Input devices
Data can be entered into the computer's memory by a variety of devices discussed later in this book. Some of the main input devices are:

keyboard	mouse
operator's console	light pen
Optical Character Reader (OCR)	digitiser
punched card reader	bar code reader
Magnetic Ink Character Recognition (MICR)	

Output devices
In order that the results of processing can be understood and used by humans it is necessary to *print*, *display* or *dump* the contents of memory using one of the following:

Visual Display Unit (VDU)	laser printer
line printer	graphics display unit
dot-matrix printer	graph plotter
daisywheel printer	sound
signal to control machinery	

Backing storage

Since the contents of main store memory are lost when the computer is switched off, *backing storage* is needed to save the contents permanently. The most common forms are *magnetic tape* and *magnetic disk*. Both programs and data files are permanently saved on magnetic storage media then retrieved or loaded into main memory when needed.

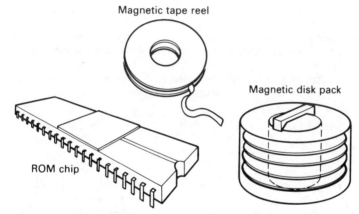

Fig. 1.11   *Storage of programs*

ROM

ROM is similar to backing storage on disk or tape except that the contents of ROM cannot normally be altered. Frequently-used programs may be *burned* onto chips as an alternative to magnetic disk. These ROM chips are plugged inside the computer, giving security and rapid retrieval of programs. ROM chips can only be programmed once and thereafter only *reading* of their contents is possible – hence the name ROM, i.e. *Read Only Memory*.

Hardware

This term means the physical components of the computer, made from metal, plastic, silicon, etc. Hardware includes all the components mentioned earlier, i.e. the central processor, keyboard/operator's console, and the peripheral units such as printers and disk drives. All computers also include pieces of hardware called *interfaces*.

Interfaces

An interface is a device, usually consisting of *integrated circuits*, which enables peripheral units to be connected to the central processor. These include disk drives and printers. Special programs are also needed to complete the interface.

A *modem* (*modulator/demodulator*) is an interface which connects a computer to the telephone network. Digital signals leaving the computer are converted to analogue signals by the modem, to permit transmission along the telephone lines. Similarly, the modem permits analogue data to be received and converted to digital data for input to a computer.

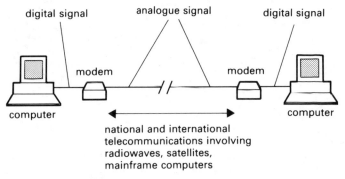

Fig. 1.12   *The modem: an interface to link computers*

Microprocessor-controlled devices

The previous notes describe the use of *microprocessors* as the centre of a complete computer system including peripheral devices such as keyboard, screen and printer. Microprocessors are also built into devices such as washing machines, televisions, cookers, cars and central heating. The microprocessors in these devices are generally unseen by the user and control the device according to pre-programmed instructions stored on ROM chip.

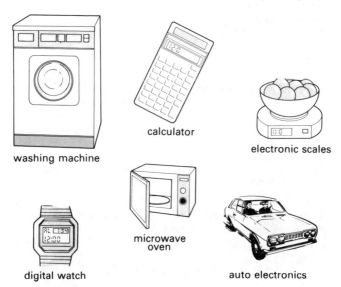

washing machine

calculator

electronic scales

digital watch

microwave oven

auto electronics

Fig. 1.13 *Devices controlled by microprocessor*

Software

Software is the programs which control the actions of the computer. There are several types of program:

1 The **user's own programs** – usually typed in at a keyboard then saved on magnetic disk.

2 **Applications packages**: Programs bought 'off-the-shelf' to do a particular task. Applications packages cover tasks such as *payroll*, *graphics*, *desktop publishing*, *stock control*, *wordprocessing* and *accounts*.

3 **Systems software**: This is the software supplied with the computer and essential for its operation. Systems software is usually supplied on disk or ROM chip and consists of *operating systems*, *compilers* and *utilities*. These are discussed later in this book.

1 State the three sizes of computer. For each give one example of a typical user.

2 Name the three parts of the Central Processing Unit.
(LEAG Specimen Paper 3, Qu. 1)

3 Give *two* examples of backing storage. State why backing store is necessary.

4 A device connected to a mainframe computer to allow input and output is known as a . . . . . .

5 Which of these is true?
A Main store can contain both programs and data.
B Variable data is normally held in ROM.
C Program instructions are normally copied to the arithmetic and logic unit.
D The contents of RAM are preserved when the computer is switched off.
(SEG Specimen Paper 1, Qu. 35)

6 Explain the difference between RAM and ROM.

7 Why are computers known as two-state systems?

8 Name an *interface* fitted to a microcomputer.

9 Give an example of a situation where a portable computer could be used and a normal desktop microcomputer could not.

10 Draw a three-box diagram to show the three main phases of any computing operation. For each phase give *two* examples.

11 (*a*) What is the relationship between a bit and a byte?
(*b*) Briefly describe the method used to store characters in a computer.
(WJEC Specimen Paper 2, Qu. 14)

12 Name three things which a byte stored in memory could represent.

13 Give *one* example of each of the following:
(*a*) hardware
(*b*) software

14 Give *one* example of each of the following:
(*a*) systems software
(*b*) applications package

15 Devices such as a printer or disk drive, connected to the CPU, are known as . . . . units.

16 What is X in the diagram below?

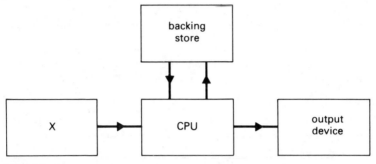

Fig. 1.14

A Graph plotter   **B** Input device   **C** Printer   **D** Visual display unit

(SEG Summer 1988, Paper 1, Qu. 6)

THE INPUT PHASE
2.1 Data capture and preparation **2**

The input phase is the collecting of data (*data capture*), followed by entry into the computer's memory. In some applications, e.g. when carrying out a survey, the data must be collected manually by filling in standard forms. In other cases the data is stored on either a magnetic or a punched medium which can be read automatically.

The entering or *loading* of data from backing storage such as magnetic disk or tape and receiving data via a modem are also part of the input process, but these methods are treated separately elsewhere in this book.

Data capture
Manual data capture involves filling in standard forms by hand. The forms are designed to show the exact layout required for entry to the computer.

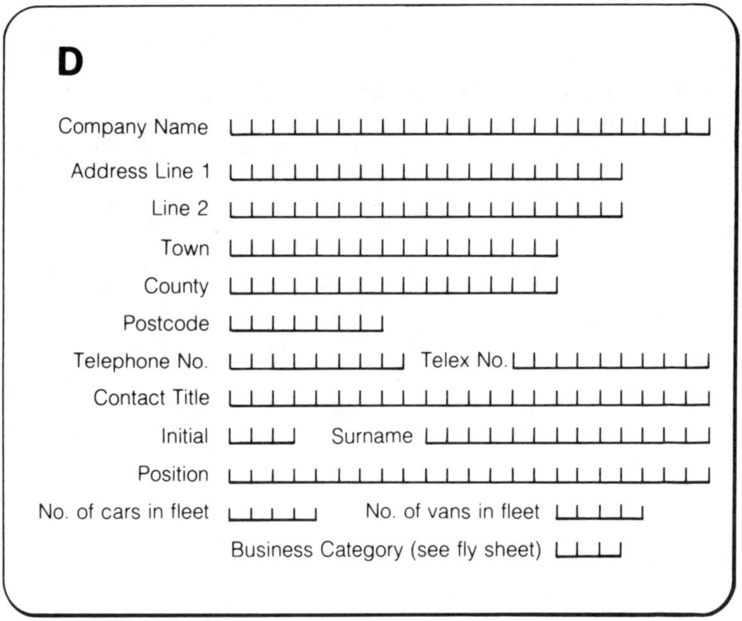
D

Company Name

Address Line 1

Line 2

Town

County

Postcode

Telephone No. Telex No.

Contact Title

Initial Surname

Position

No. of cars in fleet No. of vans in fleet

Business Category (see fly sheet)

Fig. 2.1 *The data capture form*

Coding data
Codes are used to speed entry of the data into the computer, e.g. 02 might be the code for 'one-man businesses'.

BUSINESS CATEGORIES

01 PROFESSIONAL/PARTNERSHIPS

02 ONE MAN BUSINESSES

03 RETAILERS/PUBLIC HOUSES/SHOPS

04 LEISURE/TOURISM/SPORTS

Fig. 2.2 *The coding of data*

Data preparation

Key-to-disk
The sheets of paper containing data for input to a computer are known as *source documents*. When a large number of source documents have been collected the data is usually typed via a keyboard in the *key-to-disk* system. In this system the data is typed directly onto a magnetic disk device, separate from the computer on which it will be processed. Several key-to-disk stations may be connected to a minicomputer, saving time on the mainframe computer on which the data is eventually processed. Key-to-disk is also known as *Direct Data Entry (DDE)*.

Verification
To prevent copying errors when data from source documents is entered, a second operator re-keys the same data. The two versions of the typed data are compared and any differences are signalled, so that corrections can be made by the second operator.

Validation
During the key-to-disk process, the data may be checked or *validated* by a special program to ensure that it is:

1 of the correct type, e.g. date in 6 digits dd/mm/yy;
2 within the correct range, e.g. secondary pupils' ages between 11 and 18 years.

The difference between *verification* and *validation* should be clearly understood:

> **Verification** checks for accuracy in *copying* from one medium to another.
>
> **Validation** checks that data is of the correct *type* and within a *sensible range*.

Both validation and verification help to ensure the *integrity* of the data, i.e. that the data is both *complete* (no items missing) and *accurate*.

Numerical methods
Numerical data can be checked at the entry stage by various methods in which the numbers are totalled before and after entry to the computer. The totals themselves may be quite meaningless, but any difference in the totals indicates an error in data entry. These methods include *hash totals* and *control totals*, and are discussed later together with the *check digit*. This is a digit calculated from an existing number for checking purposes, e.g. divide a bank account number by 11 and take the remainder as the check digit. Every time the account number is entered (along with the check digit) the computer calculates a new check digit and compares the two.

Keyboard

On microcomputers, the keyboard is used to enter the data directly into the computer's memory for processing prior to *saving* on magnetic disk. Most keyboards have about 100 keys laid out in a standard format, starting with the letters QWERTY.

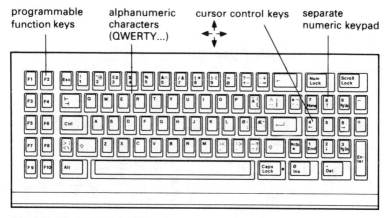

| programmable function keys | alphanumeric characters (QWERTY...) | cursor control keys | separate numeric keypad |

Fig. 2.3   *The QWERTY keyboard*

The *keyboard operator* needs to be a competent *touch typist* if large quantities of data are to be entered; untrained typists waste a lot of time searching for keyboard characters – the 'hunt and peck' method. An extra set of digits on the right of the keyboard (the numeric key pad) is provided for the entry of large quantities of numbers. Keyboard operators are also known as *VDU operators* and are part of the data preparation staff.

Operator's console

A computer operator uses an operator's console for controlling a mainframe computer. This involves tasks such as starting and stopping the computer, loading new disks, printing on paper, etc. The console consists of a special keyboard and VDU (screen); the operator responds via the console to prompts and signals from the CPU.

The mouse or WIMP system (Windows, Icons, Mouse, Pull-down menus)

The *mouse* is used instead of a keyboard for certain operations. It is moved around a flat surface, at the same time moving a large ball-bearing on its underside. This causes electrical signals which move a *pointer* on the screen.

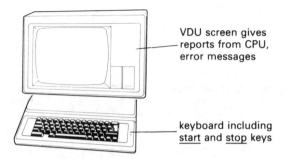

Fig. 2.4   *The operator's console*

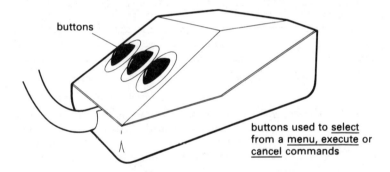

Fig. 2.5   *The mouse*

Shapes on the screen known as *icons* represent various computing operations, such as saving or loading disk files or printing on paper. To select an operation the pointer is moved to the correct icon, and a button on the mouse is pressed to execute the operation.

As the pointer is moved around the screen, various additional sets of icons appear, usually from the top of the screen. These are known as *pull-down menus*. A popular WIMP system is GEM, made by Digital Research.

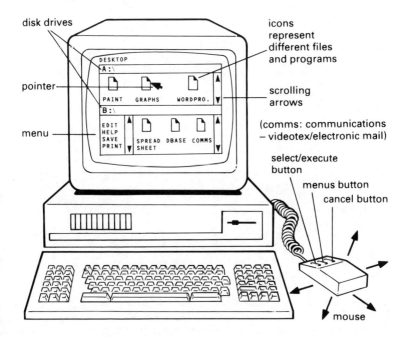

Fig. 2.6 *A 'WIMP' user-friendly operating system*

The main advantage of the mouse is that the operator doesn't have to learn complex operating commands to be typed at the keyboard. However, data such as numbers and letters must still be entered via the keyboard.

Painting with a mouse
A further use of the mouse is with a *graphics* or *paint* program, to produce pictures on the screen which can be saved on disk or printed on paper. Apart from 'freehand' drawing and painting, *standard shapes* such as a circle or an ellipse can be selected. The shapes can be *enlarged*, *infilled* with colour or *moved* around the screen. Various 'drawing tools' may be selected, such as a *paintbrush* or *pencil*. Text can be combined with graphics to form a single document.

Fig. 2.7   *Painting with a mouse*

Desktop publishing

This is one of the fastest growing applications of computers. A mouse and WIMP microcomputer system is used to replace many of the traditional page design and artwork processes. Many different fonts (or styles of lettering) can be called up on the screen and headlines can be specified to produce newspaper/magazine-style documents. The package also allows drawing with the mouse and the incorporation of digitised photographs in the text. If the computer output is sent to a laser printer, very professional results can be obtained; for example, advertising leaflets, school or parish magazines. One of the pioneers of desktop publishing was the Apple Macintosh microcomputer.

Advantage of the mouse

- Easy to use, with very little training: enables computers to be used by non-experts in a 'user-friendly' fashion.

Disadvantages

- Cannot be used for entering numeric or text data.
- Requires special software, e.g. for drawing.
- Not very accurate for drawing.

A *joystick* (or *games paddle*) is similar to a mouse, but uses a central lever to control objects on the screen, e.g. in a *computer game*, a *flight simulator* or *graphics* program.

Light pen

This is about the size of a normal pen. It is used to point to objects on the screen. When the pen is close to or touching the screen, a button on the pen is pressed and the computer detects the position of the pen. The pen may be used to select items from a menu, to draw lines or standard shapes, or to modify an existing drawing.

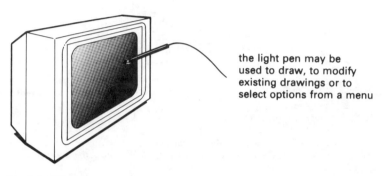

the light pen may be used to draw, to modify existing drawings or to select options from a menu

Fig. 2.8 *The light pen*

The light pen is very easy to use but like the mouse cannot be used for the entry of text or numbers.

The *touch sensitive screen* is used in a similar way to the light pen and screen. The finger is used to point to objects or icons on the screen and to make selections from menus.

Digitiser (or graphics tablet)

A drawing is stored in the computer's memory as a set of *x,y coordinates*. To do this the drawing is traced using a hand-controlled device known as a *puck*. The puck has a fine cross-wire to enable the drawing to be traced with great accuracy. The *graphics tablet* is marked out by a grid of wires, in squares similar to graph paper. This enables the exact position of the puck to be located as it moves around the drawing, while the coordinates are entered into memory automatically. The puck usually incorporates several keys which enable the user to select commands from a menu on the tablet.

Once the picture has been stored in the computer's memory it can be displayed on the screen and very easily modified using a light pen, before reprinting. This is much faster and easier than modifying drawings by hand. The digitiser is particularly useful for *architects*, *designers* and *draughtsmen/ women* (*CAD* or *Computer Aided Design*).

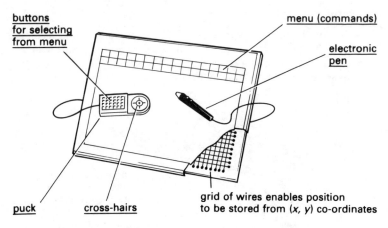

Fig. 2.9   *Digitiser (graphics tablet). Used for:*
1 'freehand' drawing with pen
2 modifying existing drawings in memory
3 digitising existing pictures from paper, using the puck for accuracy

Apart from the hand-operated devices mentioned in the previous section, there are a number of methods where *machine-readable* cards or documents can be input directly to a computer. These media can be classified as:

Optical: Bar codes, optical characters, mark sensing
Magnetic: Magnetic Ink Character Recognition (MICR), magnetic stripe
Punched: Punched card, punched tape, Kimball tag

Optical input media

Mark sensing or Optical Mark Reading (OMR)
Pencil marks are placed in boxes on data capture sheets or cards, using a soft (HB) pencil. The computer detects the *graphite* in the pencil lead. The documents may take the form of *multiple choice examination papers*, *hospital meal orders*, or cards for the *recording of time* spent on different tasks by employees of large companies.

Mark sense documents can be filled in by a person without special training. The *optical mark reader* can enter the data relatively fast.

The disadvantage is that the documents can be affected by grease, dirt and creasing.

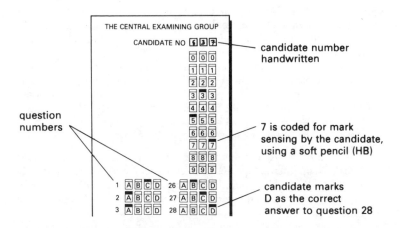

Fig. 2.10 *Mark sense document – multiple choice examinations*

Bar codes

These are widely used in supermarkets and factories. Bar codes can be printed on adhesive labels, on plastic badges or as part of a printed document, e.g. a book cover. Plastic bar codes can be attached to components during manufacturing, e.g. car or electronic parts. The main purpose of bar codes is to provide unique *identification* of items; this enables data to be collected which is useful to sales and production management. The data stored in the bars may include codes for *country* of origin, *manufacturer* and *product*, e.g. 138 might be baked beans.

Fig. 2.11   *A bar code*

The bar code is a set of vertical bars and spaces; each character (usually digits 0–9) is represented by a pattern of several bars and spaces. The characters are printed in normal text next to the bar code. Most bar codes represent *numeric* characters only, e.g. the European code *EAN*. The American code *'3 of 9'* represents 43 characters consisting of numbers, letters and signs.

A hand-held *wand* reads a bar code as its tip is passed along the length of the code. The bar code can also be read by a *laser scanner* which may be up to one metre away (e.g. in a point-of-sale (POS) terminal in a supermarket). Laser scanners may be hand-held or built into the POS terminal.

Advantages of bar codes

- Easy to use – only a few minutes' training is needed. Bar code scanning is fast, so supermarket queues at checkout counters (POS) are reduced. Data is automatically entered to the computer for *stock control/re-order* purposes; management receive information on sales or production of different items.
- Bar codes are versatile; they can be applied to many types of product and are not easily damaged by dirt or heat.

Disadvantages

- They cannot be used for variable data (e.g. prices), only for the identification codes of a particular item.
- The code must be printed on a flat surface.

Optical Character Recognition (OCR)
The *OCR reader* can interpret characters printed in a *standardised font* or style of lettering, which has been stored in the computer. Ordinary type-written or printed characters and even hand-written text may be recognised but with less speed and accuracy.

The text is scanned by a bright light and the characters are projected onto a screen containing a large number of *photo-electric sensors*. This enables the computer to identify areas of black or white; comparison with the standard characters stored in the memory allows the characters to be identified.

The London clearing banks have agreed on a set of *OCR characters*: *OCR.B Size 1* is frequently used in large commercial enterprises such as banking. The recognisable character set is:

```
0 1 2 3 4 5 6 7 8 9
A P V X / & %
```

Note: the modified zero shown above must be
used whenever possible.

Fig. 2.12 *Optical character recognition: specification for optical characters used by National Girobank*

Turnaround document
A turnaround document is used as both computer output and input. It is a form produced by a computer, using perhaps a line printer, laser printer or dot-matrix printer. The document may include certain fixed data printed in OCR characters. It is used to record *variable data*, e.g. electricity or gas meter readings, perhaps by using pencil marks for mark sensing. The document is then re-submitted to the computer, which 'reads' both the pre-printed data and the new data.

Optical character readers are fast and accurate. The data can be read by both people and computers.

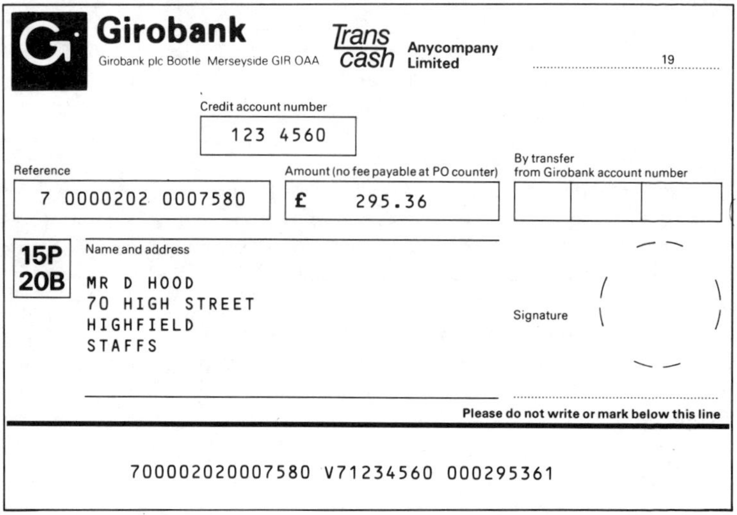
Girobank
Girobank plc Bootle Merseyside GIR OAA
Trans cash
Anycompany Limited
19
Credit account number
123 4560
Reference
7 0000202 0007580
Amount (no fee payable at PO counter)
£ 295.36
By transfer from Girobank account number
15P 20B
Name and address
MR D HOOD
70 HIGH STREET
HIGHFIELD
STAFFS
Signature
Please do not write or mark below this line
700002020007580 V71234560 000295361

Fig. 2.13 *A turnaround document*

Magnetic input media

Magnetic Ink Character Recognition (MICR)

These are special characters printed on documents such as bank cheques. They are printed in a special ink containing ferric oxide. The cheque is input to an electronic reader and the characters are automatically magnetised. The magnetic signal given off by each character varies in strength according to the shape of the character; this enables the character to be identified by the computer.

Fixed details such as the cheque number, branch number and account number are pre-printed on each cheque. Variable data, i.e. the amount of money to be paid, is encoded in magnetic ink by a special machine in the branch at which the cheque is presented.

Advantages of MICR

- MICR is accurate and fast (2000 documents per minute).
- MICR is secure (difficult to forge), not easily damaged.

Disadvantages

- Equipment is expensive, very large quantities of documents are needed to justify the expenditure.

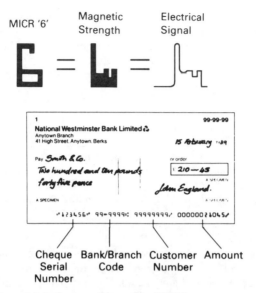

Fig. 2.14 *Magnetic Ink Character Recognition (MICR)*

Magnetic stripe cards
These are usually plastic material. A strip of magnetic tape is mounted on the card; the tape is divided into a number of *tracks* on which both numbers and letters may be encoded. The cards may be read by a special *magnetic stripe reader* or a *hand-held scanner*. Typical applications are for bank/credit cards and for personal identification cards in large organisations.

strip of tape holding machine-readable data

Fig. 2.15 *The magnetic stripe card*

(Identification cards are usually referred to as magnetic badges.) Magnetic stripes are also used on phone cards which replace cash in some telephone kiosks operated by Mercury Communications. (British Telecom phone cards are read and updated using lasers.)

Magnetic stripe cards are fast, easy to use and provide a secure form of data input.

Cash cards

Bank 'cash cards' are used to obtain cash and some other banking services outside of normal banking hours, through a 'hole in the wall'. The customer account is identified by the magnetic stripe, together with a *Personal Identification Number (PIN)* which must be keyed in. These cash dispensers (*Automatic Teller Machines – ATMs*) are connected to the bank's main computer, saving cashiers' time and enabling accounts to be rapidly updated.

EFTPOS

A new application of the magnetic card is *Electronic Fund Transfer At Point of Sale (EFTPOS)*. A shop customer wipes the card across the reader and enters his/her Personal Identification Number. The computer checks the customer's bank account and if there is enough money the amount is deducted and transferred to the shop's bank account. This is all done electronically between banks, using the telephone network. No cash changes hands (the 'cashless society'), and there is less clerical work needed by the shop and the banks. The risk of theft is also reduced.

The magnetic stripe card may eventually be replaced by the *Smart Card* now being evaluated by banks and other institutions. This is a small plastic card containing a microprocessor and memory; a person's financial situation or entire medical history could be stored. Reading and alteration of the data is only possible using a special terminal, so security and privacy of the data is ensured.

Punched input media

The punched input media (cards and tape) are now considered old-fashioned and are only used in some specialist applications such as the clothing and shoe industries.

Punched card

Punched card is one of the earliest forms of data input media, dating back to the Jacquard loom of 1801. In many computing applications the punched card has been superseded by more modern methods such as key-to-disk. The punched card normally consists of 80 columns, each column representing one character (letter of the alphabet, etc.). The data is also displayed as *alphanumeric text* across the top of the card (*interpreting*). Data is punched by a *key punch operator* using a separate *off-line machine* (not connected to the computer). A second operator verifies the data by repunching the same card on a different machine. Any difference in the keys pressed signifies an error.

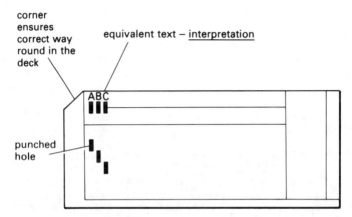

Each character (A, B, C, etc., 0–9,; ! etc.) is represented by a vertical column. There are 80 columns per card, consisting of 2 holes (letters), 1 hole (digits), 3 holes (punctuation marks). The holes represent 1s, no hole 0s, to form <u>binary codes</u> for each character.

Fig. 2.16   *The punched card*

There are normally 12 rows, characters being encoded by punching out one, two or three holes at each of the 80 vertical positions or *frames*. Each of the digits 0–9 requires only one hole to be punched, each letter of the alphabet two holes, while other characters and punctuation marks may be represented by three holes.

A light scans the card in the card reader. Light passing through the holes in the card is detected by *photo-electric cells* which convert the pattern of holes into binary pulses for input as bytes to the memory.

Advantages of punched cards

- Quite resistant to dirt and creasing.
- Good readability.
- Cards can also be read by humans (if interpreted).
- An error can be corrected (or a modification made) by repunching a single card.

Disadvantages

● In factory environments, grease can cause reading errors.
● Easily dropped so that the correct order is lost.
● Punched cards are bulky, and must be carefully stacked in a large input hopper, forming a 'queue' with other decks of cards waiting to be processed.

Punched tape
Punched tape is very similar in principle to the punched card, except that the tape is continuous. Letters, digits and punctuation marks, etc., are encoded in the same way, each character position being known as a frame.

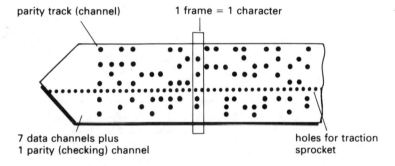

parity track (channel)   1 frame = 1 character

7 data channels plus   holes for traction
1 parity (checking) channel   sprocket

Fig. 2.17 *Punched tape*

The main disadvantage with tapes is that an error requires the whole tape to be repunched. An advantage is that the tape is physically smaller than a pile of cards and data cannot become misplaced. Paper tape is cheap.

Kimball tag
A Kimball tag is a small *punched card* commonly attached to items of clothing in shops. A main feature is that the data for a particular garment, e.g. style, size, colour, appears as both punched holes and as printed text which can be read by customers.

The Kimball tag may be read by a point-of-sale terminal and the details stored on a magnetic cassette tape. Alternatively, the Kimball tags can be collected and taken to the main computer department where they are input as a batch – *batch processing*. This enables the computer stock files to be updated for re-ordering, and provides information for management, e.g. on best-selling lines.

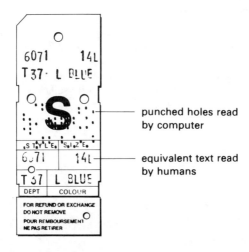

punched holes read
by computer

equivalent text read
by humans

Fig. 2.18 *The Kimball tag (a miniature punched card)*

Advantage of Kimball tags

● Kimball tags save time – no keying in of data is needed.

Disadvantages

● The cards can be torn.
● The data cannot be changed – price cannot therefore be included.

An input system of the future – voice recognition

Computers cannot, at the moment, recognise normal, fluent speech; this is
far too varied and complex with so many different dialects and meanings.
However, it is possible to 'train' a computer to recognise a limited number
of commands spoken by a particular person. Prior to using the system for a
particular task, the required set of words is spoken by the user and recorded
by the computer for future reference.

This is useful in situations where it would be difficult to enter data using a
keyboard; for example, on a car assembly line, on the floor of a warehouse
or by handicapped people unable to use their hands. The words must be
spoken very slowly and carefully, by the person responsible for the original
recording. Once a word has been 'understood', the associated command
can be carried out.

The central processor of a digital computer works with *binary* data – 0s and 1s. Most physical processes in the real world are controlled and monitored by *measuring parameters* such as temperature and pressure. These vary *continuously*, whereas the computer works with separate or *discrete* numbers. The temperature must, therefore, be *sampled* at regular intervals.

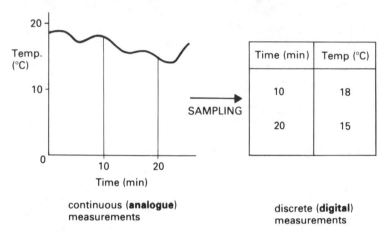

SAMPLING

Time (min)	Temp (°C)
10	18
20	15

continuous (**analogue**) measurements

discrete (**digital**) measurements

Fig. 2.19

Similarly, the hands on a mechanical or 'clockwork' watch move continuously, while a digital watch displays a set of digits – representing a discrete sample of the time every second.

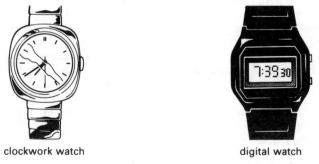

clockwork watch

digital watch

Fig. 2.20

Monitoring and control

Many applications require analogue quantities to be controlled and monitored by computer. These include chemical processes, e.g. food manufacture, monitoring of pressures in oil pipelines (testing for cracks, blockages), and patients' heartbeat. All of these processes operate in *real-time*, i.e. the data is input to the computer continuously and if necessary the computer responds immediately with a control signal. This may be necessary to lower the temperature in a furnace or to correct the proportion of ingredients in the manufacture of chocolate.

The measurements are made by *sensors*, which enable quantities such as pressure and temperature to be represented as *voltages*. The *analogue-to-digital* converter changes the voltages to binary digits acceptable to the Central Processing Unit (CPU).

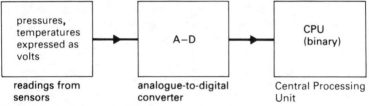

Fig. 2.21 *Analogue-to-digital conversion*

Feedback

The control program contains the parameters or acceptable limits of the process being monitored, e.g. temperatures. If these are exceeded, the computer sends a signal to the *control devices* (switches, valves, etc.) to bring the process back within limits. This action will produce new parameters which are returned as input to the computer for monitoring and possible further control action. The continuing cycle whereby *output* signals are sent from the computer and produce further *input* responses is known as *feedback*.

Fig. 2.22 *Feedback*

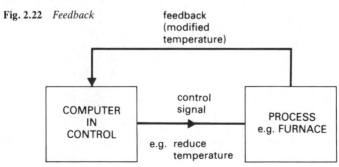

Analogue–digital devices

The *mouse*, *light pen* and *joystick* are examples of analogue devices used with microcomputers (which normally have a built-in analogue–digital converter). The *modem* mentioned previously is an A–D converter, receiving *audio signals* (analogue) and converting them to digital signals for input to the computer.

Input method	Typical applications	Comments
Keyboard (including key-to-disk)	Entry of text and figures in wordprocessing, spreadsheets, databases. Copying from source documents	Typing skill necessary for large quantities of data
Operator's console	Controlling a mainframe computer	Contains keys for tasks such as starting and stopping the computer
Mouse	Operating software by selection from menus (WIMP), e.g. wordprocessing. Also for drawing and painting, selecting different fonts	Easy for novice to use. Cannot enter text or figures. Special software needed. Large flat area needed for movement of the mouse
Light pen	Drawing, selecting from a menu; reading bar codes	Similar to mouse but pen is pointed at the screen. Special software is needed
Touch sensitive screen	Selection from a menu by pointing at required items with the finger	Not as precise as the mouse or light pen
Digitiser/graphics tablet	Storing technical drawings, modifying and reprinting in design (CAD), architecture	Easy to use, faster than traditional drawing methods
Mark sensing/ OMR (Optical Mark Recognition)	Manually completed forms, e.g. hospital meals, exam scripts, job/time recording	Easy to fill in (with pencil), correct mistakes. Batch processed. Used for variable data
Bar codes	Library books, supermarket items, factory components for identification purposes. Read by light pen ('wand') or laser beam at POS (point-of-sale) terminal	Easily read, fast, provides stock and sales information. Only fixed data
Optical Character Recognition (OCR)	Standard forms used in commerce, banking, gas and electricity bills. Turnaround documents can be used for both output and input	Read by both humans and computers. Most efficient with standardised fonts
MICR (Magnetic Ink Character Recognition)	Bank cheques for account number, branch number and cheque number	Fast, accurate, secure. Fixed and variable data (encoding)

Magnetic stripe cards	Credit cards, cash cards (for Automatic Teller Machines (ATM)). Electronic Fund Transfer at Point of Sale (EFTPOS). Phone cards, medical case history	Secure. Used with PIN. Reduces handling of cash
Punched card/tape	An outdated medium previously the main input medium for mainframe computers in data processing, e.g. payroll, scientific and engineering calculations	Batch processing. Cards awkward to handle, bulky. Largely replaced by key-to-disk
Kimball tag	Small punched cards used in clothing stores	Can be read by machine and by humans
Voice recognition	Stock control, use by the physically handicapped. Wordprocessing in the future	Limited to a finite number of 'learnt' words. Versatile systems some years away
Analogue input	Monitoring processes involving physical measurements, e.g. pressures, temperatures represented as voltages. Chemical/food manufacturing, oil pipelines, patients' heartrate, greenhouse temperature, robot control, etc.	Analogue measurements converted to binary by analogue-to-digital converter for entering to CPU
Joystick/games paddle	Controlling the movement of screen objects in computer games	Easy to use. An example of analogue-to-digital conversion

THE INPUT PHASE
Sample questions

2

1   Name *six* distinct devices for computer input.
(NEA Specimen Paper 1, Qu. 2(a))

2   Give *one* reason why an artist might prefer to use a mouse rather than a keyboard.
(LEAG Specimen Paper 1, Qu. 16)

3   Choose *two* devices from the given list to complete the sentence.

games paddle   graph plotter   bar code reader   bus ticket

A . . . . and a . . . . are both computer input devices.
(MEG Specimen Paper 1, Section G, Qu. 6)

4   MICR and OCR are methods of data input.
   (*a*) State *one* application which uses MICR.
       Why is MICR used in this application?
   (*b*) State *one* application which uses OCR.
       Why is OCR used in this application?
   (*c*) Give *one* disadvantage of both these methods of input.

5   State an advantage to the management of a supermarket chain of using a POS (point-of-sale) terminal rather than an ordinary till.
(MEG Specimen Paper 3, Section B, Qu. 6)

6   What is the function of unit X in the diagram?

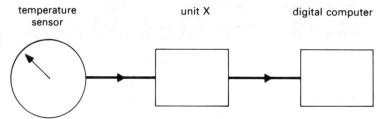

Fig. 2.23

   A Digital-to-analogue conversion
   B Verification
   C Feedback
   D Analogue-to-digital conversion

(SEG Specimen Paper 1, Qu. 19)

7   A clothing shop uses POS (point-of-sale) terminals. What is an appropriate method of data input to the terminal? Give reasons for your choice.   *(MEG Specimen Paper 3, Section B, Qu. 3)*

8 Choose *one* device from the given list to complete the sentence.

magnetic ink character reader   document reader
bar code reader   graphics tablet
point-of-sale (POS) terminal

The most appropriate input device for use in reading a code printed on a library borrower's card would be a . . . .
(MEG Specimen Paper 2, Section D, Qu. 2)

9 Which of these is an important principle of control technology?
  A Verification   **C** Validation
  B Feedback   **D** Compilation
(SEG Specimen Paper 1, Qu. 6)

10 In a program a menu of choices is displayed on the screen. Select one of the following input devices which you consider to be suitable for the user to choose an item from the menu, and give reasons for your choice.

joystick   bar code reader
keyboard   optical character reader
key-to-disk

(MEG Specimen Paper 2, Section C, Qu. 10)

11 List *three* items of data which would be input to an EFTPOS system.
(MEG Specimen Paper 1, Section G, Qu. 8)

12 In a paint sprayer there is a pressure sensor which measures the pressure of the paint as it leaves the nozzle. This sensor produces a continually changing voltage. Why does the data from the pressure sensor have to be changed before the computer controlling the paint sprayer can use it?

(MEG Specimen Paper 3, Section A, Qu. 13)

The output phase is the communication to a user of the contents of the computer's memory. This will frequently be in the form of text, pictures (graphics), sound or a signal to control machinery. If a permanent record is needed then *printout* on paper (*hard copy*) is needed; if it is enough simply to see the results of processing for a short time then a *Visual Display Unit (VDU)* is used, e.g. for checking the balance in a customer's account in a bank.

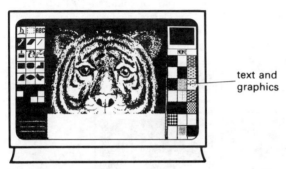

text and graphics

Fig. 3.1   *The VDU or monitor*

A VDU (also known as a screen or monitor) is based on a *cathode ray tube* similar to a television. Data being input via a keyboard also appears on the screen and may be edited.

Text
The VDU screen may be either *coloured* or *monochrome* (e.g. green letters on a dark background) and the quality and clarity of the output depends very much on price. For continuous wordprocessing a high quality VDU is necessary to reduce *eye-strain* and *health problems* resulting from small

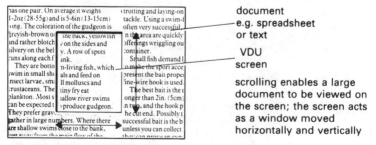

document
e.g. spreadsheet
or text

VDU
screen

scrolling enables a large document to be viewed on the screen; the screen acts as a window moved horizontally and vertically

Fig. 3.2   *Scrolling a large document*

quantities of radiation emitted. The normal text screen is 80 columns across (i.e. 80 characters per line) with about 25 lines down the screen. Much larger documents than the screen can be displayed, e.g. a *spreadsheet* with 8000 columns, by using the screen as a '*window*' and *scrolling* the text past.

Graphics

The most common screen used with microcomputers is the *raster scan* which divides the screen into *picture elements* or *pixels*. These are squares which may be addressed individually as *x*, *y* coordinates. Different modes are available, in which the choice of colours may be traded against the number of pixels available, since mapping the screen uses memory. In *high resolution graphics* the screen may be typically 1000 × 1000 pixels but the extra memory used may mean fewer colours are available. Close examination of the screen shows that these pictures are made up of small squares. A copy of the raster scan graphics display is usually made on paper using a *dot-matrix printer* and a suitable *screen dump* program.

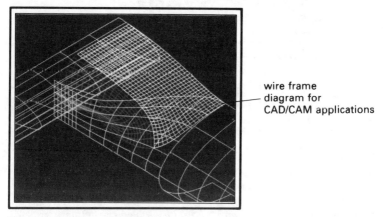

wire frame diagram for CAD/CAM applications

Fig. 3.3 *Computer graphics*

For professional graphics work, e.g. design of engineering components (CAD), a more accurate display known as *vector graphics* is used. This produces finer lines, without the jagged edges of the pixels given by the raster scan. A copy of a graphics screen can be produced on paper using a special *graphics plotter*.

The VDU is used in virtually all computing applications, from the mainframe operator's console and the supermarket point-of-sale terminal (POS) to the minute LCD (Liquid Crystal Display) on portable computers.

Advantages of the VDU

- Permits interactive computing, where the computer produces an immediate response to the user. The screen may be used as both input and output, e.g. when selecting items from a menu with a mouse, or modifying a drawing with a light pen or digitiser/graphics tablet. Information retrieval, e.g. to check if an item is in stock, will produce an immediate output on the screen.
- The VDU is fast, silent and is usually very clear and attractive compared with paper.

Disadvantages

- There is no permanent record of the output.
- There is some evidence of health risks, such as headaches and eye-strain.

The output from the VDU is not permanent, and there are many applications where the output needs to be studied away from the computer. In many cases only *hard copy*, i.e. printout on paper, is satisfactory. Such applications include:

- gas and electricity bills
- wages slips
- engineering designs used on the factory floor
- plans of buildings used on site
- advertising leaflets circulated by post
- letters produced on a wordprocessor
- authors' texts sent to publishers

Different types of paper are used:

Continuous stationery is perforated to allow separation into single sheets. Holes down the side allow the paper to be moved on by a *tractor feed* (pulled by sprocket wheels). For high quality work, **single sheets** are normally used; this is moved through the printer by friction against a roller.

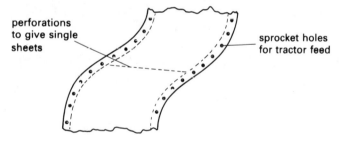

perforations to give single sheets

sprocket holes for tractor feed

Fig. 3.4 *Continuous stationery*

Pre-printed stationery is used for high volume applications such as gas bills and payslips. The paper is already laid out with headings and boxes, and the computer is programmed to print the *variable data*, e.g. the amount owed, in the correct boxes on the form. This is quicker and cheaper than printing the complete form each time.

Printer interface
Data travels from the computer via a cable, either:

- in parallel – Centronics-type interface
- in serial – RS 232 interface

A 08C BANK OF SCOTLAND MONTHLY PAYROLL SAMPLE   PAY DATE 30/05/86

MRS   D L MACLEOD   COST CODE **ACCTS**   PAY STN. **001** NO.   **15T**

	HOURS	GROSS PAY	AMOUNT	DEDUCTIONS	AMOUNT
TAX PERIOD 12	169.00	BASIC PAY	500.00	INCOME TAX	119.70
TAX CODE 176L		OVERTIME	20.00	NAT. INSURANCE	51.03
PERIOD HOURS 169.00		BONUS	20.00	PENSON	20.00
RATE 0 295.857		C/OUT	9.00	S/LIFE	12.50
RATE 1		W/END	18.00	RENT	36.00
RATE 2				S/CLUB	2.50
RATE 3					
HOL.CR					
THIS PERIOD					
TO DATE					
B/F C/F		OTHER GROSS PAY		OTHER DEDUCTIONS	
CAT NAT. INS. No. A OT885520A	169.00	TOTAL PAY ➡	567.00	TOTAL DEDUCTIONS ➡	241.73

ANNUAL SALARY	PENS. CONT. TO DATE	STATUTORY SICK PAY		'ER. NAT. INS.		
		TO DATE	THIS PERIOD	THIS PERIOD		⬇
6000.00	180.00	0.00	0.00	51.03		

TAXABLE PAY TO DATE	TAX PAID TO DATE	NATIONAL INSURANCE CONTRIBUTIONS TO DATE			PAYMENT METHOD	NET PAY
		TOTAL	EMPLOYEE	CONT. OUT.		
6624.00	1456.20	1315.14	612.36		CH	325.27

Fig. 3.5   *Pre-printed stationery*

In the *parallel* interface the data travels as a set of 8 bits (byte) side by side; in the *serial* interface the bits travel in sequence (like a train).

Printer buffer

The computer or the printer may also contain a printer *buffer*. This is a section of memory which temporarily holds bytes of data sent to the printer. The buffer is needed because the printer, which is relatively slow, cannot always keep up with the output from the computer, which is much faster.

Spooling

When there are many users, running different programs, the output to the printer may be temporarily stored on disk, to wait for printing. The separate jobs form a *queue* and the process of writing printer output to disk prior to printing is called *spooling*.

Dot-matrix printer

The dot-matrix printer is one of the most commonly used for general computing work and is especially popular with microcomputers. The principle of operation is that a pattern of small pins is 'fired' against a ribbon onto the paper, as the print head moves across the paper.

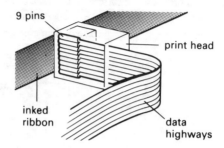

Fig. 3.6   *Dot-matrix print head*

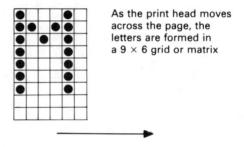

As the print head moves across the page, the letters are formed in a 9 × 6 grid or matrix

Fig. 3.7   *Printing a character*

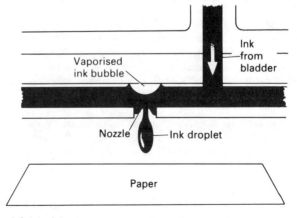

Fig. 3.7a   *Ink-jet printer*

The output from dot-matrix printers varies in quality according to their price and specification. Cheap dot-matrix printers employ only *9 pins*, so quality is poor because of the spaces between dots. Such output is only suitable for *first drafts*, etc., and for work where speed is more important than quality, e.g. invoices, delivery notes and for listings used in developing computer programs. To improve the quality of dot-matrix output, the printer may be operated in *Near Letter Quality (NLQ)* mode where the print head moves twice over every line to fill in the gaps. This reduces the printing speed to less than half the speed in draft mode. Expensive *24-pin* and *48-pin* printers are available giving much better quality and speed.

Special programs, or *printer drivers*, enable different *fonts* (styles of lettering) to be selected within a sentence, e.g. italics, superscripts (as in x^2), or subscripts (as in H_2O). Letters may be **emphasised** (made darker) to highlight certain words.

Advantages of dot-matrix

- Relatively high speed (typically 200 characters per second, but more expensive dot-matrix printers approach 500 cps in draft mode).
- Pictures (graphics) may be printed using a screen dump program.
- Relatively cheap.

Disadvantages

- Quality not acceptable for some purposes (e.g. legal documents, publishing, business correspondence).

Other types of matrix printer
Ink-jet printers are similar to dot-matrix, but instead of small needles being forced against a ribbon, *ink* is sprayed out of tiny nozzles to form characters from a series of spots. Since there is no impact the ink-jet printer is fast and quiet. A main feature is that text and graphics can be produced in many *different colours*.

The **thermal printer** uses heat-sensitive paper to produce the characters from a pattern of dots. A stylus is used instead of pins as in the dot-matrix, and this burns away the top of the paper to form the letters. The thermal printer is slow (about 30 characters per second).

Daisywheel printer
The daisywheel printer employs exactly the same design of printing mechanism as the electronic typewriter. The daisywheel consists of a complete set of characters attached to spokes around a central hub.

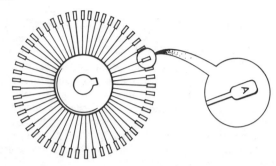

Fig. 3.8   *Daisywheel*

As the daisywheel is moved across the paper, it is continually rotated to bring the required letters into position. A complete character is printed on the paper by striking the appropriate 'petal' onto an inked ribbon.

The daisywheel printer is frequently used with a microcomputer for wordprocessing, as an alternative to the typewriter, especially when high quality output is needed, e.g. in secretarial work.

Daisywheel printers vary in price from approximately £200 to £2000.

Advantage of the daisywheel

• The main advantage of the daisywheel is that perfectly typed letters may be produced.

Disadvantages
The disadvantages include:

• The daisywheel printer is very slow (8–100 cps).
• Printing is very noisy and acoustic hoods are sometimes needed for soundproofing in an office environment.
• Daisywheel printers are the least versatile of all printers – fonts can only be changed by fitting a different daisywheel, e.g. a single word cannot be highlighted in italics in the middle of a sentence.
• Graphics or pictures are not possible.

The laser printer
This is the most sophisticated type of printer; it combines the high quality of the daisywheel with the speed and versatility of the dot-matrix. However, unlike the dot-matrix and daisywheel, which print a character at a time, the laser is a *pageprinter*, with a typical speed of 8–15 pages per minute on microcomputer systems involved in applications such as desktop publishing. IBM laser printers used on mainframe computers are capable of 20 000 lines or about 300 A4 pages of text per minute. Characters are formed from dots, but since the density may be 90 000 dots per square inch, the quality is high.

The laser printer works on the same principle as the photocopier. A page of data is received from the computer and an image written onto a drum using a laser and a *photographic toner* – the black powder used for printing. A complete page is transferred to the paper in an electrical fusion process. Then the roller is cleaned before the image of the next page is formed on the roller.

The complex nature of laser printers makes them expensive both to buy and to maintain, so the laser printer is mainly found in commercial organisations, e.g. for printing bank statements. Their high quality makes the laser printer ideal for wordprocessing leaflets and booklets (including pictures), e.g. in advertising, with a quality approaching that of the professional typesetter or printer. This use of computers, known as *desktop publishing*, is increasing in popularity, largely due to the Apple Macintosh microcomputer and Apple LaserWriter printer.

Fig. 3.9 *Desktop publishing with the Apple Macintosh*

Advantages of the laser printer

- High quality (almost as good as typesetting used in books).
- Versatile – output can be text and graphics. Many different fonts.
- Very fast and quiet – prints a page at a time.

Disadvantages

● Expensive to buy (£1500–£10 000 or more) and to maintain.

Line printers

Chain printers

A set of embossed metal characters is attached to a chain which is driven at high speed past the paper. A carbon ribbon sits between the chain and the paper. A hammer mechanism strikes each character as it passes the position(s) on the paper where it is to appear.

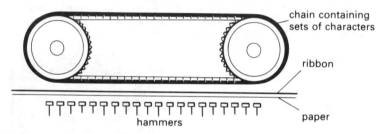

chain containing
sets of characters

ribbon

hammers

paper

Fig. 3.10   *The chain printer*

Barrel or drum printer

The barrel or drum printer is also a line printer. The barrel is covered in rows of each letter.

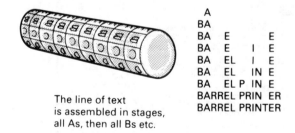

The line of text
is assembled in stages,
all As, then all Bs etc.

```
A
BA
BA   E            E
BA   E      I     E
BA   EL     I     E
BA   EL   IN E
BA   EL P IN E
BARREL PRIN ER
BARREL PRINTER
```

Fig. 3.11   *The barrel or drum printer*

To print a line, the drum rotates and as the row of As passes the printing position on the paper, all As for that line are printed by a row of electro-mechanical hammers; there is a hammer at every character position on the line. Then all Bs in the row are printed (if any) and so on through the alphabet until the complete row has been printed.

Advantages of line printers

- Line printers such as chain and barrel printers are relatively fast (up to 3000 lines of 132 characters per minute, or 6600 characters per second).
- *Complete characters* contact the paper (via the ribbon) rather than a matrix of dots. So quality can be good, although smudging is sometimes a problem.
- *Multi-part stationery* allows several copies to be made, e.g. for invoices and delivery notes. One copy is kept for accounts/records, one copy goes to despatch and another is given to the customer when the goods are delivered.

Disadvantage

- They are expensive and suitable only for large *mainframe* systems in organisations such as banks, local authorities and industrial corporations.

Plotters

The printers mentioned so far are not generally used for the output of technical drawings such as house plans or engineering designs. For this work a special *plotter* is used which consists of a single *pen* whose movement on the paper is controlled by the computer. The paper is held on a *flat bed* or a *drum*.

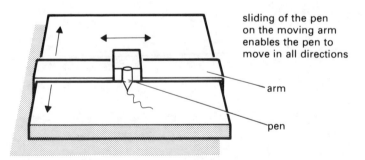

Fig. 3.12 *Flat bed plotter*

Drafting plotters can handle large rolls of paper. Very large sheets of paper can be used. The pen moves at a speed of up to 60 cm/s and text as well as drawings can be printed.

A complete CAD (Computer Aided Design) system would include a digitiser/graphics tablet with puck, light pen and VDU for input, connected to a micro, mini or mainframe computer, using the plotter for output. In large organisations the CAD system has replaced the traditional drawing board equipment of pencil and paper.

Fig. 3.13 *The Hewlett-Packard drafting plotter*

Computers may be used to control machinery. The *binary data* leaving the computer must be converted to an *analogue signal* such as voltage, by a digital-to-analogue converter.

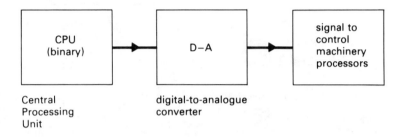

Fig. 3.14 *Digital-to-analogue conversion*

Monitoring and control

Many applications fall into the category of monitoring and control of processes. A pipeline carrying oil may be monitored by measuring pressure and temperature; any deviation from safe limits, e.g. due to a crack in the pipe or a blockage, would result in a control action from the computer. This might be a *warning signal* (perhaps on a VDU) or a signal to shut the system down.

The control output could also activate levers or electric motors, e.g. to open or close greenhouse windows to optimise the temperature. In an automatic dairy farm the computer senses when milking has finished and automatically removes the milking apparatus or cluster from the cow. The computer also monitors each cow and delivers the correct amount of feed for that particular animal.

Computer Aided Manufacture

Computer Aided Manufacture (CAM) uses computers in the making and assembling of engineering products. *Computer Numerically Controlled (CNC)* machines, such as lathes, manufacture parts according to a set of instructions programmed on a tape – replacing the skill of a manual operator (*craftsman*) by the skill of a *programmer*.

CNC – Computer Numerically
Controlled

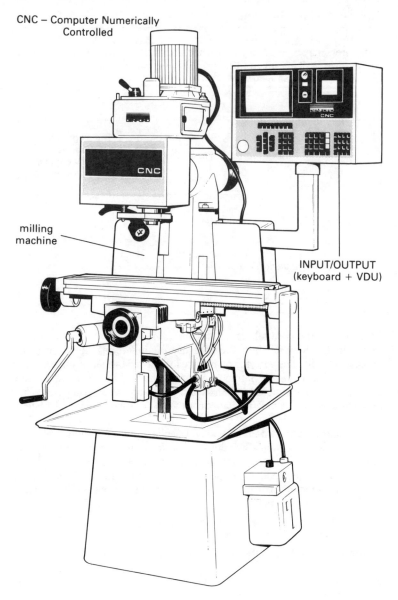

milling
machine

INPUT/OUTPUT
(keyboard + VDU)

Fig. 3.15   *Computer Aided Manufacture (CAM)*

Robotics

Robotics includes the use of computers to control welding machines and paint sprayers used in the manufacture of cars, etc.

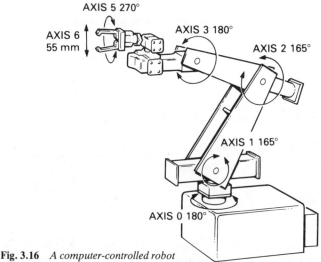

Fig. 3.16 *A computer-controlled robot*

Robots are extremely accurate, reliable and able to work in extreme conditions of heat, cold, fumes and danger (e.g. bomb disposal, mini submarine).

Real-time

Control applications operate in real-time: conditions are monitored by sensors and suitable response signals are output immediately, i.e. without delay. This is necessary in monitoring all types of manufacturing processes and also when *controlling vehicles*, e.g. the direction of a rocket or the timing of traffic lights. In the *car engine management system*, sensors monitor the amount of fuel, temperatures and pressures; the computer analyses these and then makes automatic adjustments to give the best performance in terms of power, fuel economy and reduced pollution.

A *route guidance system* helps drivers to make journeys across busy cities. The grid reference of the destination is fed into an on-board computer. Along the route the driver is guided by speech output from the computer, which monitors and controls the car relative to a number of *beacons* attached to traffic lights. Communication between the car and the beacon is by either *infra-red beams* or *microwaves*. Information also appears on a small screen on the dashboard. This is a real-time application since the signals must be sufficiently prompt to make frequent route adjustments in heavy traffic possible.

Computer output on microfilm (COM)

This is a very compact method of storing data which has been output from a computer; the screen output is *photographed* and then reduced in size by a factor of either 24 or 48.

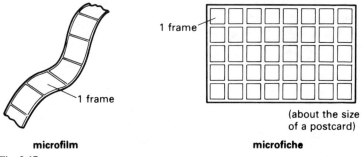

Fig. 3.17

When the pages or *frames* are arranged in the form of a grid the film is known as a microfiche. The frames are magnified by placing in a viewer or *microfiche reader*. The fiche can be scrolled to bring the required frame into view.

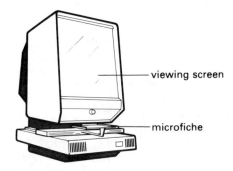

Fig. 3.18 *Microfiche reader*

A single sheet of microfiche 6 inches × 4 inches can store 250 pages of A4. Microfiche is therefore used wherever storage space is at a premium. Common uses of microfiche include the *archiving* of large quantities of data in a compact form, for example library book details, bank statements, car spares, service instructions for electronic appliances.

Speech and sound

Speech synthesis is in its early stages, but systems exist which can produce recognisable sound from text entered via a keyboard. A document could be produced on disk on a wordprocessor and then listened to by a blind person. Speech output is also used for giving *warnings*, e.g. to tell a driver if his/her seatbelt is not fastened.

Music synthesisers are now used by pop musicians because of the ease with which various instruments can be *simulated* and complex rhythms programmed.

Output method	Applications	Comments
VDU (screen/monitor)	Interrogating a database, checking items in stock. Playing a computer game. Wordprocessing, newspaper production, editing, spreadsheets. POS terminal. Warnings from monitoring and control. Viewing drawings, Computer Aided Learning (CAL) or Programmed Learning	No permanent record. Fast, quiet, may be monochrome or colour
Dot-matrix printer	Draft work, bills, invoices, wage slips, program listings, accounts, spreadsheets	Poor quality but fast, versatile (various fonts). Graphics (drawings) screens may be 'dumped'. Relatively cheap
Daisywheel printer	High quality letters, reports, legal, professional work	Slow, noisy, but quality as good as a typewriter
Laser printer	Wordprocessing, leaflet publishing, advertising, bank statements, bills	Versatile, high quality but expensive. Ten times faster than older impact printers, e.g. chain
Chain and barrel printers	High volume use for bills, bank statements, etc. Local authority rates on mainframe computers	Fast, good quality, very expensive
Plotters	Computer Aided Design (CAD) where accurate drawings are needed, replaces draughtsman e.g. design and architecture	Much faster and more accurate than traditional drawings. Modifications to drawings made easily
Thermal printers	Were extensively used on cheap home computers	Special metallic paper needed. Cheap but slow
Ink-jet printers	Similar to dot-matrix. Printing of graphics, artwork	Various colours may be printed. Quiet
COM	Libraries, banking, spare parts records	Very compact form of storage

Control signals	Robotics, Computer Aided Manufacture (CAM), control of traffic lights, pelican crossings, milking parlour, car performance, vehicles (rockets), car routes, monitoring patient's heartrate, temperature	Fast, accurate, reliable, tolerates dangerous conditions, e.g. noise, heat, pollution, etc. Operates in real-time
Sound	Speech synthesiser, useful for disabled – instead of braille. Emergency warnings, electronic music	Early stages of development

1   Name *four* distinct devices used for computer output.

(NEA Specimen Paper 1, Qu. 2(b))

2   A small business plans to buy a microcomputer system including two printers to cover all of their requirements. For each application suggest a suitable type of printer and give a reason.
(*a*) Printing invoices, delivery notes, payslips.
(*b*) Printing important letters.

3   An office manager is installing a computer system and must decide between:

a matrix printer; a daisywheel printer; a line printer

Which of these would you expect to
(*a*) be cheapest, (*b*) be fastest, (*c*) be most versatile, (*d*) produce best quality reports?

(NISEC Specimen Paper III, Section B, Qu. 38)

4   Which of the following is a control application?
   A producing payslips
   B maintaining customer files
   C designing a bridge
   D running a motor at constant speed
   E information retrieval

(NISEC Specimen Paper III, Section A, Qu. 30)

5   A firm's computer installation has the following peripheral devices, in addition to the console:

visual display units, microfilm camera (used for COM), line printer, graph plotter.

State which devices are likely to be used by the following people and give reasons for your particular choices.
(*a*) A clerk, using an on-line stock control system, wishing to see if there is a particular spare part in stock.
(*b*) The sales manager wishing to send each day by post to each of the firm's 50 branches an up-to-date statement showing the spares held at the main depot. (There are generally several thousand items in stock.)
(*c*) The accounts department wishing to produce payslips for each employee in the firm.

(NEA Specimen Paper 2, Qu. 9)

6   Give *two* reasons for using pre-printed stationery for computer output.

Give an example of an application where pre-printed stationery is used.
(NISEC Specimen Paper III, Section B, Qu. 39)

7   Large quantities of output can be produced on microfilm or by a printer.
    (*a*) Give *one* advantage of using a printer rather than microfilm.
    (*b*) Give *one* advantage of using microfilm rather than a printer.
    (*c*) Describe *one* application which uses a printer. Why is a printer used
         in this application?
    (*d*) Describe *one* application which uses microfilm. Why is microfilm
         used in this application?

(LEAG Specimen Paper 3, Qu. 18(b))

8   Briefly describe an application which uses a digitiser for input and a
    graph plotter for output. Explain why each component is so appropriate
    for this application.

(LEAG Specimen Paper 3, Qu. 18(c))

The need for backing storage

The contents of the computer's memory (immediate access store) are lost when the computer is switched off – the memory is said to be *volatile*. Any important data or programs which will be needed in future must be *saved* or *recorded* on a suitable medium. *Backing storage* is the name given to any medium on which the contents of the memory can be permanently stored for subsequent re-entry (loading). Backing storage enables programs and data files to be transferred between computers. Programs which are bigger than the computer's memory can be processed by loading and running in small sections; in this piecemeal approach the small program modules are called *program overlays*.

Recording on disk

The thin metal or plastic disk is coated with a magnetic material for the recording of data; this is achieved by magnetising spots on the surface in different directions. Disks permit very fast access both for *writing* (recording) or *reading* (retrieving) data.

Disk format

The disk is divided magnetically into a number of concentric rings or *tracks*, and radially into a number of *sectors*. This process is known as *formatting*. The computer can access any *file* (or set of data) stored on a disk by 'knowing' the track and sector number at which the file starts. Access for both reading and writing is obtained using a *read/write head*. The ability to move straight to the start of a particular file is known as *direct* or *random* access.

The disk is rotated at high speed, e.g. 3600 rpm, by an electric motor, the complete unit being known as a *disk drive*.

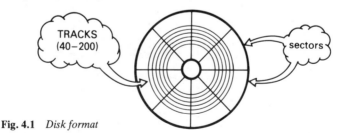

Fig. 4.1 *Disk format*

Hard disks

Disk packs

Mainframe and minicomputers use large disks (around 14in diameter);

several disks are arranged in a *disk pack* around a central spindle. The disk pack may be *fixed* or *exchangeable*. There may be several hundred tracks per disk and upper and lower surfaces of each disk may be used for recording (apart from the top and bottom surfaces of the pack).

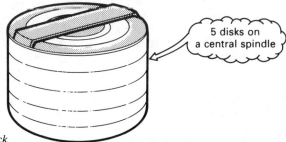

5 disks on a central spindle

Fig. 4.2 *Disk pack*

The disk is accessed for reading and writing by a read/write head. The read/write head may be either *fixed* – in which case one head is needed for each track – or *moving*, in which case the read/write head moves in and out to access the required track. *Data transfer rates* may be as high as 3 million bytes (characters) per second.

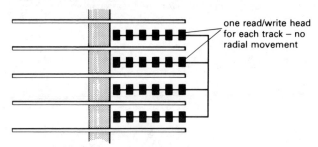

one read/write head for each track – no radial movement

Fig. 4.3 *Fixed head disk drive*

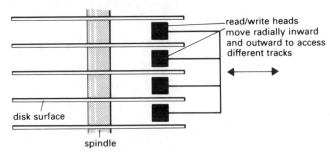

read/write heads move radially inward and outward to access different tracks

disk surface

spindle

Fig. 4.4 *Moving head disk drive*

One disk pack may have a storage capacity of 500 megabytes. Large mainframe computers used in banks, building societies or at the Driver and Vehicle Licensing Centre might have over 100 gigabytes, i.e. 100 billion characters of *Direct Access Storage Devices (DASD)*.

Typical applications of disk packs are for large organisations, e.g. gas board (customer accounts, payroll), universities (student records, project/research work), banks (accounts statements), industrial organisations (engineering, design, sales, accounts, invoices), airline booking systems, local authority (rates, social services, accounts), Police National Computer (PNC).

Winchester disk drive

This is a small 'hard' disk pack with several disks sealed in a dust-free box. It is not exchangeable. The disk is usually either 3·5in or 5·25in diameter with about 300 tracks per surface. The disk is made to a high degree of accuracy in aluminium, coated with magnetic oxide. The disk rotates at about 3600 rpm and the read/write heads float within a few millionths of an inch of the disk surfaces. Since any dust might cause a '*head crash*', possibly ruining large quantities of important data, the disk pack is sealed and not accessible to the user.

Hard disks are very popular in business, since although physically small, they permit rapid transfer of data for saving or retrieving files, together with high capacity (20–100 megabytes). Hard disk is about ten times faster than a floppy disk.

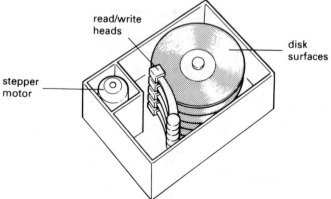

Fig. 4.5 *Winchester hard disk drive*

The Winchester hard disk may be adequate to store all the files of a small business, school or college. Since the disks themselves are sealed and not physically accessible or replaceable, any failure in the drive may lead to the loss of the entire database. Therefore regular *backing up* of files, perhaps on a weekly basis, should be practised, using a *floppy disk* or high capacity *tape streamer cassette*.

Typical users of the Winchester disk are small businesses (word-processing, database, spreadsheet, etc.); also schools and colleges, as the centre of a *Local Area Network* for students' project work or for CAL (Computer Assisted Learning) software.

Security of hard disks
Both the disk pack on mainframes and minicomputers, and the Winchester disk drive on microcomputers, are used as the backing store for networks, i.e. a large number of terminals with access to the disk drive. This can have a *security risk* for important files such as confidential records or students' project work. Therefore, hard disks require an efficient management system with *passwords* to prevent unauthorised access to files. Also, to guard against possible accidental (or malicious) damage to files, regular backing up or copying to tape should be carried out. This is also known as *archiving*.

The floppy disk (or diskette)
This is a single, flexible disk intended for microcomputers. Early floppy disks were 8in diameter, followed by the 5·25in disk which is now most common. The 3·5in disk is steadily taking over and is likely to be the standard in the 1990s.

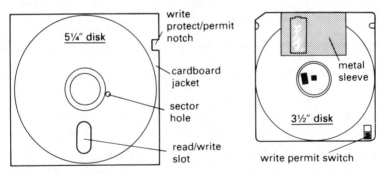

write protect/permit notch

5¼″ disk

cardboard jacket

sector hole

read/write slot

metal sleeve

3½″ disk

write permit switch

Fig. 4.6 *Floppy disks*

The principles of the floppy disk are similar to the hard disk except that the disk consists of only two surfaces. Various formats are available but an *80 track double-sided disk* is common, storing 720K of data. The latest 3·5in disks can hold 1·44 megabytes of data (1440K).

Each surface has nine sectors with 512 bytes per sector. In *soft sectored* disks the sectors are defined by a formatting program (or *software*). In *hard sectored* disks the sectors are marked by physical *holes* in the disk, detected by the disk drive (*hardware*).

Capacity of floppy disk

The capacity of each surface = $80 \times 9 \times 512$ bytes.

For a double-sided disk:

Capacity = $2 \times 80 \times 9 \times 512$
$= 737\,280$ bytes

$1K = 1024$ bytes

Therefore disk capacity = $737\,280 \div 1024 = 720K$.

IBM disk capacities

	Single sided	Double sided
40 track	180K	360K
80 track	360K	720K

Floppy disks must be formatted using a special *utility program* supplied by the manufacturer. This magnetises the new disk in the correct layout of tracks and sectors for the particular brand of computer. The most common disk format for floppy disks is the *IBM format* which has been applied to very many different makes of microcomputer. This enables disks (and programs) from one make of computer to be used in other makes of machine. This '*IBM compatibility*' dominates business computing.

Applications of floppy disks

Floppy disks are the most common medium for the purchase of software (programs) for microcomputers. These include the *operating system*, e.g. MSDOS. They are light and may easily be transported by post.

A minimal microcomputer business system would have twin floppy disks – some programs require two disks '*on-line*' simultaneously. Copying (backing up) is faster with twin disk drives. A more powerful combination is to have one floppy disk drive and one Winchester hard disk drive.

The floppy disk is used for wordprocessing, accounts, spreadsheet work, desktop publishing, small database files, educational programs (CAL) and games. As the price of Winchester hard disks continues to fall the floppy disk will be used more for transportation and back-up of software rather than as the main direct storage medium.

Many microcomputers are now supplied with disks which enable them to *emulate* or 'impersonate' an IBM machine; this enables disks in the IBM format to be used. Examples of computers which can use emulators are the

Acorn Archimedes and the Atari ST. The reason for the emulator is that there are already several thousand programs available on disk in the IBM format. *IBM-compatible* computers are quite different from software emulators; compatibles are built with similar components to IBM machines, thus giving hardware *and* software compatibility.

For home and educational use (e.g. in schools) the floppy disk is fast in relation to the cassette tape sometimes used. Compared with the Winchester disk, however, both the capacity and data transfer rate of the floppy disk are poor.

The main disadvantage with floppy disks is that their capacity (720K) is not enough for many applications, so that large collections of disks requiring careful storage and labelling soon accumulate. In business use most new software (programs) is transferred to Winchester hard disk, with the floppy being used for backing up important files or for transferring files between computers, e.g. by sending disks through the post.

Security of floppy disks
Data can be corrupted if the disk is left near to a magnetic source. The 3·5in disk is more robust than the 5·25in disk and has a built-in *write-permit switch*.

Data on a 5·25in floppy disk can be protected from accidental damage by sticking on a *write-protect tab*, which makes the disk READ ONLY until the tab is removed. Floppy disks may be re-used repeatedly for recording new data.

Magnetic drum
This is a mainframe storage medium and works in a similar way to the magnetic disk pack – except that data is stored in parallel tracks around the drum surface, which is coated in magnetic material.

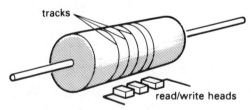

Fig. 4.7 *Magnetic drum storage*

The magnetic drum is now considered old technology, but provides a fast access storage medium for some applications, e.g. *information retrieval* from databases. The drum is physically very large (about 1 m long) and the associated equipment expensive.

Advantages of disk drives (all types)

- Access is fast for saving and retrieving files.
- Very large amounts of data can be stored in a small space, compared with traditional files, i.e. on paper.
- Direct or random access permits files to be accessed immediately without reading through other files.
- The disk surface can be used repeatedly by overwriting new data.
- Sophisticated '*housekeeping*' operations are possible, e.g. delete files, update records, rename files, catalogue files, etc.

Disadvantages

- The disk drive units themselves are expensive compared with alternative methods.
- Computer programs to handle certain types of random access disk files are more complex than programs for alternative forms of storage (e.g. sequential files on tape).

Disks are now the main medium for information retrieval systems – when answers are needed quickly, e.g. interrogating the Police National Computer (PNC) for details of a suspected stolen car; enquiring about a customer's bank account or gas bill. The airline booking system needs to be permanently up-to-date, i.e. operating in real-time, otherwise the same seat could be sold to two different people. This is only practicable with a disk system – a tape system would be too slow and does not permit direct access.

Reel to reel tape

The *magnetic tape reel* is about 10in in diameter and contains up to 2400 feet (370 m) of tape 0·5in wide.

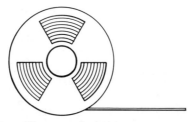

Fig. 4.8   *Magnetic tape reel*

The tape is a plastic material coated with a magnetic oxide; spots can be magnetised to indicate a 1 or a 0. The spots are arranged in nine *tracks* or channels, eight tracks for the binary code for each character and one channel as a *parity* check. Even parity means that a frame will always have an even number of 1s; if the code for a character has an odd number of 1s then the parity bit will be 1 to make the total even. This is checked when the tape is read – when even parity is used an odd number of 1s indicates an error.

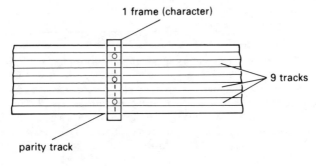

Fig. 4.9   *One frame on magnetic tape*

The density at which bytes (characters) can be stored or packed on the tape varies up to about 6250 bytes per inch, giving a maximum capacity for one tape reel of 180 megabytes. Data may be transferred to the CPU at up to 2·5 million characters per second.

The tape is threaded through a series of rollers or *capstans* which allow high speed winding and re-winding past the read/write heads. The loops of tape in each vacuum tube are held in place by suction. This prevents the tape breaking on starting or stopping.

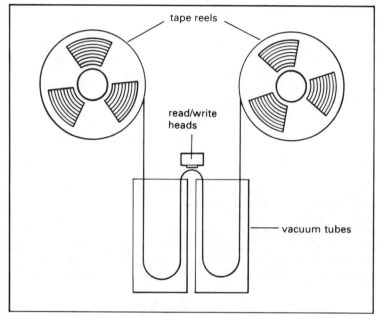

Fig. 4.10   *Magnetic tape read/write*

Magnetic tape is not as fast as magnetic disk for either read or write operations, but considerably faster than punched cards. It is still widely used for the compact storage of large data files – an organisation can store hundreds of tapes very compactly in racks, to form a *tape library*, e.g. a large bank might have 5000 tapes. The storage capacity of a magnetic tape is normally very much larger than the memory in the CPU (Immediate Access Store). Large files may need to be processed in several stages by loading blocks of data from tape into memory – each new block *overwriting* the previous contents of memory.

Magnetic tape reels are especially suitable for archiving data from disk and are particularly easy to transport. A computer operator must ensure that the correct tape is loaded and this is confirmed by a *header* on the tape. *Inter-block gaps* between sets of records or individual records allow time for the starting and stopping of the tape. An *end-of-file marker* indicates the end of a set of records.

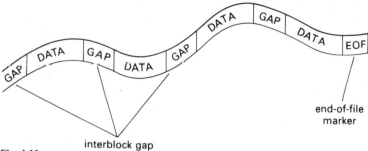

interblock gap

end-of-file
marker

Fig. 4.11

Advantages of magnetic tape

- It is cheaper than magnetic disk.
- It is very compact and easy to transport.

Disadvantages

- Random or direct access to files is not possible.
- Individual records cannot be modified/updated.

Apart from its use for archiving data held on disk, there are some applications where tape is quite adequate, i.e. where files don't have to be accessed and updated in real-time. Suitable examples for tape are where a large number of records can be processed *sequentially* (*batch processing*), i.e. one after the other. Examples are the weekly preparation of payslips, the marking of mark sense examination papers.

Cassettes

These are similar in principle to magnetic tape but much smaller (the same size as an audio cassette). The main uses include the storage of games, etc., on home computers and as a medium for transferring data to mainframe computers from *point-of-sale (POS)* and bank *cash point* terminals. The cassette is too slow for many purposes.

Cartridges

A *cartridge* is a small tape designed especially for backing up disks – very high data transfer rates are possible (up to 2·5 Mb per second) and also much greater storage capacities (30 000 bytes per inch). The cartridge is only a quarter of the size of a tape reel, measuring $4 \times 5 \times 1$ inches, but can store more data.

The cartridge drives require less cleaning than the tape reel drives, and being physically smaller, cartridge libraries are much more compact than equivalent tape reel libraries.

Tape streamer

This is a small cassette designed for back-up for the Winchester hard disks used in microcomputers. Typical capacity is 20 Mb, with a data transfer rate of 5 Mb/minute.

KEY FACTS
The differences between random and serial access

Random or direct access

This is only possible with magnetic disk. Random access involves moving to a file (or record within a file), without first reading through all preceding files or records on the disk. Individual records can be changed without re-writing the entire file.

Serial or sequential access

This is the only method possible with tape-based systems. Serial access requires all preceding files, or records, on a tape to be read in order to access an individual file or record. Serial access does not allow individual records to be updated – the entire file must be written to a new tape to include the changes.

Strictly speaking, ROM is not backing storage but has been included in this section since it can be used for storing programs as an alternative to the usual storage media, i.e. disk or tape. However, as a form of *permanent storage*, it differs from disk or tape in that the user cannot normally alter the contents. The ROM is usually programmed by the manufacturer, for example with a wordprocessor program or the computer operating system and programming languages.

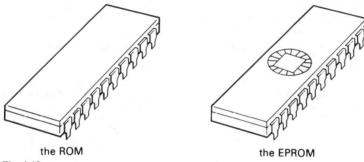

the ROM   the EPROM

Fig. 4.12

The contents of the ROM are permanently 'burned' onto the chip and cannot normally be altered – hence the name *Read Only Memory*. The user cannot save programs and data on it, as with disk or tape. Typical software stored on ROM are the computer *operating system* and *utility programs* necessary for the running of the computer. These are collectively known as *systems software*. A frequently used *wordprocessor* may also be supplied in ROM instead of disk. An example is the View ROM for the BBC Micro.

A *PROM* is a ROM chip which can be programmed once by the user – *Programmable Read Only Memory*.

An *EPROM* – Eraseable, Programmable, Read Only Memory – can be wiped clean and reprogrammed using a special device known as an *EPROM 'blower'*.

Advantages of ROM chips

- The program is more secure than on a disk, which may be lost or damaged.
- Loading is very much faster than disk.

Disadvantages

- Contents may not easily be altered – cannot 'write' to it.

- Software tends to be more expensive on ROM chip.
- ROM 'slots' in the computer are finite in number.
- Fitting and removing not as convenient as disks.

CD-ROM – optical disk

The *compact disk* is a new medium which enables huge amounts of data to be stored. The disks vary in size from 3·5in diameter holding 150 megabytes of data (or 75 000 typed pages) to a 12in disk with a capacity of about 1000 megabytes or 500 000 pages.

The disk is written to and read from by a laser beam, which detects small pits in the surface of the disk by the way light is reflected. As in many computer storage media, the binary digits 1 and 0 correspond to the presence or absence of a pit. An alternative method is to use the laser to magnetise spots on the disk in certain directions. Data transfer rates are very high.

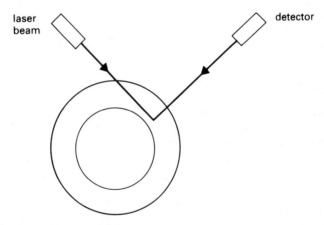

Fig. 4.13 *Compact or optical disk*

The compact disk is a form of ROM (Read Only Memory), since once the contents are written, they cannot be altered. This makes the medium most suitable for applications where fixed, unchanging data is to be archived, e.g. in libraries or files of company records. A major application under consideration is the use of CD-ROM as an alternative to the printed book – already complete volumes of encyclopaedias have been stored on one disk. In commercial applications, the read only nature of the compact disk gives good security – for example, financial records cannot be altered.

However, unless it becomes possible to alter the data, the CD-ROM will not replace the magnetic disk as a versatile form of read/write storage. The

WORM (Write Once Read Many times) is a form of CD-ROM which allows the user to write once on a new blank compact disk.

CD-ROM allows the storage of pictures and sound as well as text, one application being *interactive video*. These enable educational and training material to be manipulated by the student, using a microcomputer. This gives the student far more control than a video tape to access a particular item. The equipment to read CD-ROM is currently quite expensive.

KEY FACTS
The differences between RAM and ROM

RAM   Random Access Memory – the main store used for holding the user's own programs and data. Contents may be repeatedly overwritten (changed) by the user.
        Contents of RAM are *volatile* – lost when the computer is switched off.

ROM   Read Only Memory – a chip containing permanently stored programs. May not be altered by the normal computer user, only read from. Mainly used for systems software, not the user's own programs or data.

CD-ROM A compact or optical disk used for storage of vast quantities of fixed data.

Magnetic bubble store
Bubble store is different from disk, tape and ROM. As with ROM there are no moving parts, but the medium can be both written to and read from. It is a *solid state* system.

Small bubbles on the surface of a magnetic material are magnetised in one of two directions to represent binary 0 or 1. Although no physical movement takes place, the patterns of magnetised bubbles representing bits can be transferred to the edge of the bubble store where reading and writing takes place.

Data in bubble store is *non-volatile* – the data remains after electrical power to the system has been switched off. Bubble store is faster than disk storage and physically much smaller.

Storage medium	*Applications*	*Comments*
Magnetic disk pack	Information retrieval on large mainframes, payroll, airline booking, stock control, large databases, Police National Computer, banks, building societies	Fast, high storage capacity, direct access, expensive compared with tape
Winchester hard disk	Micro and minicomputers, for business, school/college use, wordprocessing, databases, spreadsheets, programming	Faster than floppy, much greater storage capacity. Suitable for computer networks
Floppy disk	Microcomputers in the home and education, also for supplying new software, e.g. through the post. 3·5in likely to supersede 5·25in disk	Cheap, light, faster than tape cassette but lacks speed and capacity of Winchester hard disk. Direct access
Magnetic tape (reel to reel)	Mainframe computers, especially as a back-up for archive material from disk or for batch processing, e.g. DVLC, bank archives	Cheap, high capacity. Good storage and transportation. Slow access times. Only serial or sequential access
Cartridge	Likely to replace large tape reels for archiving	Very small, high capacity
Cassette	Small magnetic tape used on home microcomputers, point-of-sale terminals, cash dispensers	Cheap, compact but very slow data transfer. Only serial access
CD-ROM (compact disk)	Storing very large quantities of fixed data, e.g. encyclopaedias, books, interactive video for training, etc	High capacity, rapid direct access, very secure but data cannot be changed or updated
ROM	Fixed inside computer to provide frequently used software, e.g. languages and operating systems	Fast loading, safe and reliable. Cannot be altered or written to

1   Name two different secondary storage devices that might be used in
    (*a*) a microcomputer, (*b*) a mainframe computer.
    (WJEC Specimen Paper 1, Qu. 3(b))

2   An estate agent wishes to purchase a microcomputer system. The
    microcomputer will be used to store and retrieve details of properties
    for sale. It will also be used for wordprocessing.
    (*a*) State whether floppy disk or hard disk storage should be used and
         give a reason for your choice.
    (*b*) Which security method would be needed to ensure that property
         details held on disk would not be lost or damaged?
    (WJEC Specimen Paper 1, Qu. 13(c))

3   Files held on disk have been compared with songs held on a long
    playing record and files held on tape have been compared with songs
    held on tape.
    (*a*) Give *one* advantage of holding files on tape.
    (*b*) Give *one* advantage of holding files on disk.
    (NISEC Specimen Paper 1, Qu. 5)

4   Give two reasons for using backing storage devices.
    (NISEC Specimen Paper 2, Section A, Qu. 3)

5   Describe the following pieces of hardware and state what each is used
    for. Diagrams may be used to illustrate your answer.
    (*a*) Magnetic tape unit   (*b*) Floppy disk unit
    (NISEC Specimen Paper II, Qu. 6(a) and (d))

6   Which one of the following types of storage will *not* allow data to be
    retrieved at random.
    A main memory   **B** read only memory   **C** fixed disk
    D magnetic tape   **E** bubble memory
    (NISEC Specimen Paper III, Section A, Qu. 15)

7   A particular computer has 48K RAM (Random Access Memory) and
    16K ROM (Read Only Memory).
    (*a*) What is the ROM used for?
    (*b*) What is the RAM used for?
    (*c*) Why are both kinds of memory necessary in the computer?
    (NEA Specimen Paper 1, Qu. 9)

8   A wordprocessing package for a particular general purpose computer
    is available on disk or ROM.
    Give *one* advantage of buying a ROM chip as opposed to a disk.
    (NEA Specimen Paper 2, Qu. 6(e))

9   Name *two* direct access storage devices.

(LEAG Specimen Paper 3, Qu. 2)

10   The editor of a newspaper uses a wordprocessor for creating letters and memos. What would be the most appropriate backing store device for the wordprocessor?

(MEG Specimen Paper 2, Section D, Qu. 2)

11   (*a*)   Explain why it is *not* usually possible to transfer all the data into the CPU from a magnetic tape in one long block.
(*b*)   Information is stored on magnetic tapes in blocks separated by gaps. What are the gaps for?

(LEAG Specimen Paper 3, Qu. 7)

12   A wordprocessing package is too large for the whole of it to be held in main store at the same time as the document being processed. Explain how a backing store can be used for a program overlay in this case.

(MEG Specimen Paper 3, Section B, Qu. 4)

Two-state systems

A computer accepts data input in the form of letters of the alphabet, digits (0–9), mathematical symbols and punctuation marks. However, all internal data representation and processing is done using only the digits 0 and 1.

The digital computer is a *two-state* or *bistable* device, like a tap or a switch which can be either on or off. Within the computer, circuits are either conducting or not conducting electronic pulses; or certain voltage levels are present or absent. On magnetic storage media, spots are magnetised in one direction or another. A two-state system can therefore only represent two digits – 0 and 1. A row of light bulbs can be used to produce a range of *binary* patterns, taking an illuminated bulb to represent 1, and a bulb which is switched off to represent 0.

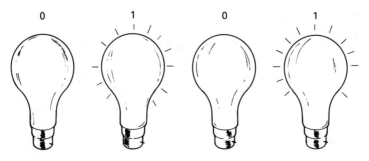

Fig. 5.1

Decimal system

The normal counting system used for manual arithmetic (with pencil and paper) is the denary or decimal system, based on the number 10. There are 10 digits 0,1,2,3,4,5,6,7,8,9 and numbers of all sizes can be represented by placing digits in various positions.

$$\times 10$$
$$\diamondsuit$$

100	10	1	
3	5	7	$(3 \times 100) + (5 \times 10) + (7 \times 1)$

The position of the digit determines its value. In this example, 3 has a higher *place value* (100s) than 5 (10s).

Binary numbers

A similar system of place values is used for the binary system, but the column values are based on 2 – this is called base 2 arithmetic.

			× 2		decimal equivalent
16	8	4	2	1	
				1	1
			1	0	2
			1	1	3
		1	0	0	4
		1	0	1	5
		1	1	0	6
				etc.	etc.

The binary system can therefore be used to represent any decimal number. The binary number is obviously very much longer than its decimal equivalent.

Decimal to binary

e.g. Convert 29 to binary.

2	29		**Method**
2	14	rem 1	Divide by 2, noting
2	7	rem 0	remainders. Continue
2	3	rem 1	until 0 in second
2	1	rem 1	column. The answer is
	0	rem 1	read from the bottom up.

This can be written as:

$$29_{(10)} = 11101_{(2)}$$

decimal (or base 10)   binary (or base 2)

Binary to decimal

e.g. Convert $101011_{(2)}$ to decimal.

1	0	1	0	1	1	**Method**

	2	5	10	21	43

Start at the left-hand digit. Double it. Add the next digit on the right. Double the result and add the next digit on the right. Repeat this across the binary digits.

Therefore $101011_{(2)} = 43_{(10)}$

The binary digits 0 and 1 are known as *bits*. It is common to work with bits in sets of 8, known as *bytes*:

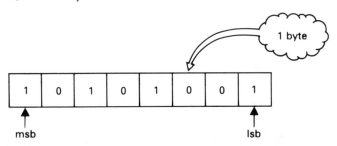

Fig. 5.2

As shown above, if the byte represents a number, the leftmost bit has the highest place value. It is known as the *most significant bit (msb)*. Similarly, the rightmost bit has the lowest value and is called the *least significant bit (lsb)*.

A *word* is a set of bits which the central processor can handle as a single unit. In microcomputers, this is often 1 byte, but in mainframe computers may be several bytes, e.g. 8 bytes (or 64 bits).

KEY FACTS

bit	binary digit (0 or 1)
byte	8 bits
word	1 or more bytes
1 kilobyte (K)	1024 bytes
1 megabyte (Mb)	1 000 000 bytes (approx.)

Store locations in memory

A simplified diagram of a computer's memory is shown below. In practice, in large computers the store locations might be two or three bytes wide. The data held in each store location might include:

- an 8-bit *code for a character* (A–Z, 0–9, etc.)
- a *mathematical number*, e.g. 54 967·37
- the *address* of another piece of data
- an *instruction*, e.g. to fetch a piece of data.

These different types of data are all stored as binary patterns and look very similar to each other. The program has the task of differentiating between characters, instructions and addresses. (This is a problem for the machine code programmer – not the user of high level languages such as Pascal or BASIC.)

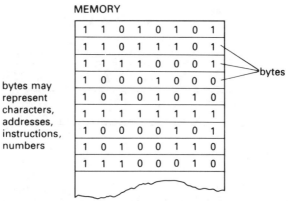

Fig. 5.3 *A section of memory 1 byte wide (large computers may use words several bytes wide)*

Addresses

The data in the memory has to be transferred to the Arithmetic and Logic Unit for calculations, etc.; the answers are then sent back to the memory. Each store location must be labelled with its own *address* for these fetching and storing operations.

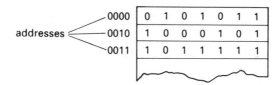

Fig. 5.4

Limits to memory size

The 4-bit addresses shown would not give a realistic memory size, only 2^4 or 16 bytes of memory. Even 8-bit addresses would only give a memory of 2^8, i.e. 256 bytes.

In practice, addresses are made up of two or more bytes (16 or 24 bits).
Memory limit using 16 bits for the addresses:

$$2^{16} = 65\,536 \text{ bytes}$$
$$= \frac{65\,536}{1024} \text{ kilobytes (K)} = 64\text{K}$$

(This is the maximum 'directly addressable' memory size of small '8-bit' microcomputers which use 16 bits for their addresses.)

Using 24 bits, the upper memory limit is

$$2^{24} = 16\,777\,216 \text{ bytes}$$
$$= 16\,384\text{K}$$
$$= 16 \text{ megabytes}$$

The addresses, using only two bytes as in small 8-bit microcomputers, would range from 0 to 65 535 inclusive (i.e. 65 536 separate addresses). In binary these would be very long numbers indeed.

	binary			decimal
0000	0000	0000	0000	0
	⟁			⟁
1111	1111	1111	1111	65 535

Machine code programmers refer to these memory locations individually.

Writing out 16-bit binary addresses is too slow and a code was devised to shorten this task. Each group of four bits (known as a '*nibble*') is represented by a single character. Four bits can produce 16 different codes.

0000	0100	1000	1100	4 bits: 16 binary patterns
0001	0101	1001	1101	
0010	0110	1010	1110	
0011	0111	1011	1111	

The set of single characters chosen to represent the 16 4-bit patterns is known as the *hexadecimal code* or '*hex*'.

Decimal	Binary	Hex	Decimal	Binary	Hex
0	0000	0	8	1000	8
1	0001	1	9	1001	9
2	0010	2	10	1010	A
3	0011	3	11	1011	B
4	0100	4	12	1100	C
5	0101	5	13	1101	D
6	0110	6	14	1110	E
7	0111	7	15	1111	F

The highest number which can be coded in eight bits is

$$1 \ 1 \ 1 \ 1 \qquad 1 \ 1 \ 1 \ 1$$

In hex, this translates to   F   F

This enables the 16-bit memory address to be represented as:

	binary				hex		
0000	0000	0000	0000	0	0	0	0
	⟁				⟁		
1111	1111	1111	1111	F	F	F	F

Instructions in hexadecimal

Hexadecimal is useful to machine code programmers, as discussed later in this book. A typical instruction would be to load data into the *accumulator*; the accumulator is a *register* or special store used for calculations.

| 1 | 0 | 1 | 0 | | 1 | 1 | 0 | 1 | *operation code* to load
the Accumulator (LDA)

In order to achieve some task the *operation code* or instruction must usually have some data to work on. The operation code is followed by one or more bytes known as the *operand*. The operand may be two bytes representing the address of another byte somewhere in the memory. This address tells the computer the location from which data is to be fetched.

The complete instruction, occupying 3 bytes of memory, would be

	instruction (operation code)		address of data in memory (operand)			
Binary	1 0 1 0	1 1 0 1	1 0 1 1	1 1 1 1	1 1 0 0	0 1 1 1
Hex	A	D	B	F	C	7

KEY FACTS

Bytes in memory may hold:

1 data, i.e. characters, numbers
2 instructions
3 addresses to fetch data from and return answers to

A byte may be used to represent characters, i.e.

Digits: 0, 1, 2, 3, 4, 5, 6, 7, 8, 9
Letters: A, B, C, . . . Z, a, b, c, . . . z
Punctuation: : , ; etc.
Symbols: = / * etc.

Each of these characters (which appear on the keyboard) must be represented by a pattern of binary digits or bits. These binary patterns or codes for characters are known as the *internal character set.*

Using only two bits, only four different bit patterns or codes can be formed; so only four characters could be represented.

bit patterns

2 bits	0	0
can give	0	1
4 codes	1	0
	1	1

Three bits would allow eight characters to be represented or 'coded'.

bit patterns

3 bits	0	0	0
can	0	0	1
give	0	1	0
8 codes	0	1	1
	1	0	0
	1	0	1
	1	1	0
	1	1	1

In fact, since the number of characters needed is over 100, a 7-bit code is used. With seven bits, since there are two possibilities (0 and 1) at every bit position, the number of different binary patterns is:

$$2^7 = 2 \times 2 \times 2 \times 2 \times 2 \times 2 \times 2 = 128$$

The 7-bit patterns range from   0 0 0 0 0 0 0
· · · · · · · · · · · · · · · · ·   128 patterns from 7 bits
to   1 1 1 1 1 1 1

ASCII code (internal character code)

A 7-bit character code has been standardised for use in computers through-out the world. It is known as the *ASCII* code, or *American Standard Code for Information Interchange.*

Character			Code					Character			Code				
A	1	0	0	0	0	0	1	0	0	1	1	0	0	0	0
B	1	0	0	0	0	1	0	1	0	1	1	0	0	0	1
C	1	0	0	0	0	1	1	2	0	1	1	0	0	1	0
D	1	0	0	0	1	0	0	3	0	1	1	0	0	1	1
E	1	0	0	0	1	0	1	4	0	1	1	0	1	0	0
. .								. .							
a	1	1	0	0	0	0	1	space	0	1	0	0	0	0	0
b	1	1	0	0	0	1	0	+	0	1	0	1	0	1	1
c	1	1	0	0	0	1	1	−	0	1	0	1	1	0	1
d	1	1	0	0	1	0	0	/	0	1	0	1	1	1	1
e	1	1	0	0	1	0	1	=	0	1	1	1	1	0	1
. .								. .							

Extracts from the ASCII Code

Parity bit

As characters are usually handled in bytes of eight bits, the 7-bit code leaves one spare bit. This is the *parity* bit, used for checking purposes.

Even parity means that every character stored should have an even number of 1s. If the code for the character has an odd number of 1s, the parity bit is set to 1 to make even parity. When data is entered into the computer, e.g. from a tape, any code having an odd number of 1s signifies an error.

7-bit code for A is   1 0 0 0 0 0 1   This contains two 1s.

So parity bit is 0   ⬚0⬚ 1 0 0 0 0 0 1
parity bit   8-bit code for A including parity bit

7-bit code for C is   1 0 0 0 0 1 1   This contains three 1s.

So parity bit is 1   ⬚1⬚ 1 0 0 0 0 1 1
parity bit   8-bit code for C including parity bit

Similarly, *odd parity* ensures that the number of 1s is always odd.

Sign and magnitude

If a byte is used to represent a positive number, e.g. 59, then there must also be a method of representing negative numbers, e.g. -17, so that useful arithmetic can be done. In the *sign and magnitude* method, the most significant bit (msb) is set at 1 to denote minus and set at 0 to denote plus. The remaining bits give the magnitude or size of the number.

```
                        sign bit 0 denotes + (positive)
   59(10) =  [0]   0  1  1  1  0  1  1(2)
  -17(10) =  [1]   0  0  1  0  0  0  1(2)
                        sign bit 1 denotes − (negative)
```

Two's complement

This method is used for the subtraction of binary numbers. The subtraction sum is converted to one of addition.

In decimal, $19 - 7$ can be thought of as $19 + (-7)$. -7 is the additive inverse of $+7$, i.e.

$$+7 + -7 = 7 - 7 = 0$$

To subtract a binary number we must first find the inverse of the number; this is called the *two's complement*.

In two's complement, the most significant bit is negative and all other bits are positive. For example, to represent the negative number -83:

-128	64	32	16	8	4	2	1
1	0	1	0	1	1	0	1

$$= -128 + 32 + 8 + 4 + 1$$
$$= -83$$

Only this bit is negative

To represent $+83$, the most significant bit is 0:

128	64	32	16	8	4	2	1
0	1	0	1	0	0	1	1

Comparing these:

	128	64	32	16	8	4	2	1
$+83$	0	1	0	1	0	0	1	1
-83	1	0	1	0	1	1	0	1

two's complement of 83

At each position except the least significant bit it can be seen that the two's complement is obtained by changing the bits of the positive number from 1 to 0 and from 0 to 1.

Method for two's complement
The complete method for forming the two's complement of a positive number in binary is shown below, using 83 as an example.

1	Write down the binary for 83.	0	1	0	1	0	0	1	1		83
2	Change all 0s to 1s and 1s to 0s.	1	0	1	0	1	1	0	0		
3	Add 1 to give the two's complement, −83.	1	0	1	0	1	1	0	1		two's complement −83

Since 83 + − 83 = 0, this can be checked:

```
  83      0  1  0  1  0  0  1  1
 −83      1  0  1  0  1  1  0  1      Two's complement
        ─────────────────────────
      [1] 0  0  0  0  0  0  0  0
```
carry bit (ignored)

Ignoring the carry bit (which the computer is also programmed to ignore), the correct answer of 0 is obtained, i.e. the two's complement method gives a true representation of −83.

Reminder: Binary Addition

0	0	1	1
+0	+1	+0	+1
0	1	1	10

Limits of eight bits
With eight bits, the highest *positive* number possible using two's complement is:

128	64	32	16	8	4	2	1	
0	1	1	1	1	1	1	1	$= 127_{(10)}$

The 'smallest' *negative* number possible in two's complement is

−128	64	32	16	8	4	2	1	
1	0	0	0	0	0	0	0	$= -128_{(10)}$

KEY FACTS
The range of numbers in 8-bit two's complement is

$$-128 \text{ to } +127$$

The overflow condition

When using a fixed number of bits, say eight, an *overflow* condition may occur when an internal carry is generated. If the eighth 1-bit were negative as in two's complement, this might be altered incorrectly by an internal carry, e.g.

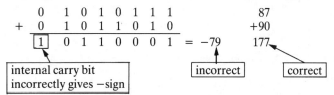

```
    0   1 0 1 0 1 1 1              87
+   0   1 0 1 1 0 1 0            +90
  ┌─┐
  │1│ 0 1 1 0 0 0 1  =  -79      177
  └─┘
```

internal carry bit incorrectly gives −sign   incorrect   correct

An overflow results when a carry bit causes an incorrect answer; the computer should detect and correct these errors.

The underflow condition

This occurs when a negative number is produced which is too small to fit into the available bits in two's complement. For example:

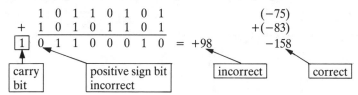

```
    1   0 1 1 0 1 0 1             (-75)
+   1   0 1 0 1 1 0 1           +(-83)
  ┌─┐
  │1│ 0 1 1 0 0 0 1 0  =  +98    -158
  └─┘
```

carry bit   positive sign bit incorrect   incorrect   correct

Storing large integers (whole numbers)

Using 8-bit two's complement numbers it is only possible to store integers in the range −128 to +127.

```
1 0 0 0 0 0 0 0    -128
0 1 1 1 1 1 1 1    +127
```

Putting two bytes together increases the range of numbers which can be represented.

```
0 1 1 1   1 1 1 1   1 1 1 1   1 1 1 1    +32 767
1 0 0 0   0 0 0 0   0 0 0 0   0 0 0 0    -32 768
```

This range of whole numbers is not adequate for many practical applications, e.g. large companies have sales in millions or billions of pounds. Larger whole numbers can be represented by putting several bytes together, e.g. 32 bits (or 4 bytes) gives a range of $\pm$ 2 billion (approx.)

Floating point
The range given by several bytes in two's complement may not be adequate for some purposes and a method of number storage known as *floating point* is needed. Floating point is used to represent both very *large* and very *small* numbers; it is similar to Standard Form employed with decimal numbers.

Number	*Standard Form*
6 398 756·0	$= 6\cdot398756 \times 10^6$
0·000 594	$= 5\cdot94 \times 10^{-4}$

In Standard Form all numbers are converted to the *mantissa/exponent* form. The *mantissa* has the same digits as the original number but with the decimal point 'floated' to give a number N such that $1 < N < 10$. The *exponent* is the power of 10.

Binary floating point
Computers use *binary floating point* to represent very large and very small numbers. The place values before and after the 'bicimal point' must be considered:

2^4	2^3	2^2	2^1	2^0	•	2^{-1}	2^{-2}	2^{-3}	2^{-4}
16	8	4	2	1	•	½	¼	⅛	¹⁄₁₆

For example:

```
   1  0  1  0  0  •  1  1  0  0
= 16 + 4 + ½ + ¼
= 20 + 0·5 + 0·25        bicimal point
= 20·75
```

In binary floating point, the binary number is expressed in mantissa/exponent form. The point is placed to the left of the first digit to give the mantissa. The exponent is the power of 2, equal to the number of places the point has moved.

```
                bicimal point        mantissa           exponent
e.g.  1  1  1  0  1  •  0  1   =   •  1  1  1  0  1  0  1  ×  2^5
```

In practice, since it is the convention that the point would always be placed on the left of the digits, the point may be omitted from floating point numbers. Similarly, since the exponent always refers to base 2, the 2 need not be stated. The binary number 1   1   1   0   1   •   0   1 can therefore be written in floating point as:

mantissa   exponent

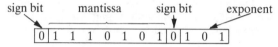

In two's complement, bits are needed for the sign, so the complete floating point number becomes:

sign bit   mantissa   sign bit   exponent

| 0 | 1 | 1 | 1 | 0 | 1 | 0 | 1 | 0 | 1 | 0 | 1 |

In large computers several bytes are used for the mantissa and several for the exponent, enabling very large numbers to be represented, suitable for most practical purposes.

Truncation and rounding of floating point numbers

Unlike the previous methods which use integers (whole numbers), floating point works on fractions ($\frac{1}{2}$, $\frac{1}{4}$, $\frac{1}{8}$, etc.). For example, convert $0\cdot3$ to a bicimal: using 8 bits this would be approximately:

| 0 | 1 | 0 | 0 | 1 | 1 | 0 | 1 |

Truncation
Using only the first four bits, $0\cdot3$ would be represented by 0100 or $0\cdot25$ decimal.

Therefore, using only four bits it is not possible to represent $0\cdot3$ accurately in floating point arithmetic. In practice, many more than four bits would be used, but errors still occur in *truncating* the answer to fit a limited number of bits.

Rounding
Using eight bits, the nearest we can get to $0\cdot3$ is

rounded up   bit used for rounding

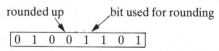

This is $0\cdot300\,781\,25$ in decimal, quite a large error relative to $0\cdot3$.

The truncated answer for four bits ($0\cdot25$) can be improved by rounding. In decimal, $3\cdot6$ would be rounded to $4\cdot0$ since it is nearer to $4\cdot0$ than to $3\cdot0$. In binary, using four bits, the 0 in the fourth position would be rounded up if the bit after it was 1. If the bit afterwards were 0, no rounding upwards would take place.

With rounding, 0·3 would become 0101 in four bits,

i.e. 0·25 + 0·0625 = 0·3125

Actual	Truncated	Rounded
0·3	0·25	0·3125

Errors using only 4 bits

1 A microcomputer uses an 8-bit word with negative numbers held in two's complement form. What range of numbers can the word represent?
A 0 to 128 **B** 0 to −128 **C** −128 to 127 **D** −128 to 128
E −128 to 255
(NISEC Specimen Paper III, Section A, Qu. 6)

2 The hexadecimal equivalent of the binary value 01100101 is
A 65 **B** A1 **C** 56 **D** 64 **E** 6B
(NISEC Specimen Paper III, Section A, Qu. 10)

3 A group of bits that are processed together is called
A a hex code **B** a record **C** a field **D** a word **E** a string
(NISEC Specimen Paper III, Section A, Qu. 28)

4 If a computer has a 6-bit word and the most significant bit is the sign bit, what is the largest positive number which can be represented?
(LEAG Specimen Paper 3, Qu. 4 part)

5 In the buffer of a particular POS terminal characters are held in 8-bit bytes before being sent to the central computer system. Each byte uses seven bits to represent the character and one bit to maintain even parity. How many different characters can this system use?
(MEG Specimen Paper 2, Section D, Qu. 1)

6 What is a bit?
A Eight bytes **B** Either 0 or 1 **C** The base for hexadecimal notation **D** The same as a word.
(SEG Summer 1988 Paper 1, Qu. 32)

7 The number −23 is stored in six bits in two's complement form as follows:

−32	16	8	4	2	1
1	0	1	0	0	1

(a) Complete the boxes with 0s and 1s to show how 27 would be stored.

(b) Complete the boxes with 0s and 1s to show how −27 would be stored.

(NEA Specimen Paper 1, Qu. 3)

8 A processor uses a 16-bit word with the first eight bits allocated to the function code and the other eight to the address. The tables show some of the function codes and the addresses of some store names in hexadecimal.

Function	Code	Store name	Address
Add	3A	X	68
Load	4B	Y	69
Store	55	Z	6A

What does 3A69 represent?

A Add X   **B** Load Y   **C** Store Z   **D** Add Y

(SEG Specimen Paper 1, Qu. 16)

9 The following diagram shows the character 'K' being transmitted down a telephone line. The system uses *odd* parity.

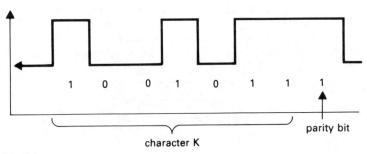

Fig. 5.5

(*a*) What is meant by odd parity?

(*b*) Why is parity used?

(LEAG Specimen Paper 1, Qu. 13)

10 (*a*) A machine code instruction can usually be broken down into two parts. Say what these are.

(*b*) What is the hexadecimal equivalent of the decimal number 90?

(*c*) Machine code instructions are represented internally in a computer in binary form. Why then are such instructions often represented elsewhere in hexadecimal form?

(SEB Ordinary Grade 1986, Section 1, Qu. 7)

Please note: Some examination syllabuses do not include logic gates; please check your particular syllabus or ask your teacher. If logic gates are not included in your examination you are still advised to read Section 6.1 briefly, if time permits, without attempting the sample questions involving logic gates.

Data bus

Computer processing involves the transmission of electronic pulses around the computer; the pulse patterns represent binary data and instructions. The routes on which the pulses travel in parallel streams are known as *data buses* or *highways*. A small microcomputer would have a data bus 8 bits wide; 16- and 32-bit data buses are common in more powerful machines.

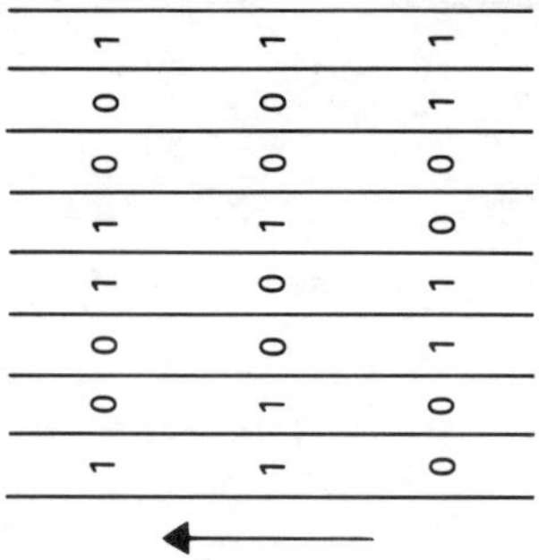

Fig. 6.1   *An 8-bit data bus*

Gates

To complete the circuits, it is necessary to have a large number of devices to control the data flow: to allow pulses to flow or not flow, to represent stored data and to perform calculations such as addition. The devices which carry out these functions are known as *logic gates* and modern integrated circuits may use hundreds of thousands of gates. These are burned onto *silicon chips* to form an *integrated circuit*. Although the gate has no moving parts, it acts like a switch in allowing pulses to flow or not flow.

Truth tables

Computers are binary or two-state devices. Many processes can be reduced to a two-state system; if a situation can be either *true* or *false* it can be modelled using 0s and 1s (1 = true, 0 = false). A simple example of the construction of a *truth table* is shown below. The table may use True and False or 1 and 0 for the two states.

Statement: Plants will thrive if the weather is warm *and* wet.

Weather		Plants
Warm	*Wet*	*Thrive*
False	False	False
False	True	False
True	False	False
True	True	True

Weather		Plants
Warm	*Wet*	*Thrive*
0	0	0
0	1	0
1	0	0
1	1	1

Statement: Some plants die if there is frost *or* drought.
The truth tables for this situation are:

Weather		Plants
Frost	*Drought*	*Die*
False	False	False
False	True	True
True	False	True
True	True	True

Weather		Plants
Frost	*Drought*	*Die*
0	0	0
0	1	1
1	0	1
1	1	1

Plants die if there is frost *or* drought. The plants would also die if there were both frost *and* drought.

The two previous examples involving plants are similar in their logic to two very important gates used in computers; the AND gate and the OR gate.

The AND gate

An AND gate is a device which takes two (or more) inputs in the form of electronic pulses.

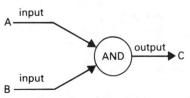

Input		Output	
A	*B*	*C*	
0	0	0	truth table
0	1	0	for the
1	0	0	AND Gate
1	1	1	

Fig. 6.2

AND Gate
1 is output if both A *AND* B are 1. In all other cases the output is 0.

The OR gate

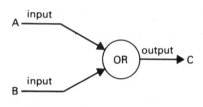

Fig. 6.3

Input		Output
A	*B*	*C*
0	0	0
0	1	1
1	0	1
1	1	1

truth table
for the
OR gate

OR gate
1 is output if *at least one* of the inputs is 1, i.e. if either A *or* B or both A *and* B are 1.

Note
This is called the *inclusive* OR gate, as it includes the case where both A and B are 1. The *exclusive* OR gate would output a 0 when A *and* B were 1.

The NOT gate
The NOT gate takes a single input and changes it. The NOT gate is also called an *inverter*.

Fig. 6.4

Input	Output
0	1
1	0

In addition to AND, OR and NOT gates there are NAND (not AND) and NOR (not OR) gates.

Gates are combined in very large numbers (many thousands) to form complete circuits. These include the *half adder* and *full adder*, which are used to add binary numbers. The half adder is used to add two binary digits, producing a carry bit and an answer bit.

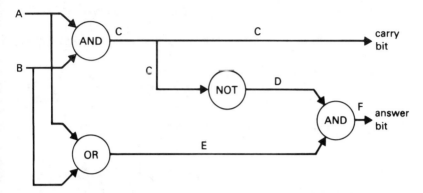

Fig. 6.5 *Circuit for a half adder*

The truth table for the half adder is drawn up by following through the circuit each of the four possible permutations or arrangements for A and B, as follows:

Inputs	
A	*B*
0	0
0	1
1	0
1	1

the four possible arrangements for inputs A and B

Note that where a single line in the circuit splits into two, the current bit (0 or 1) continues into the two separate branches.

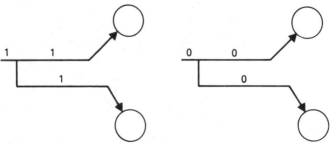

Fig. 6.6

The complete truth table for the half adder circuit becomes:

TRUTH TABLE						OUTPUT SUMMARY	
INPUT		OUTPUT			OUTPUT		
		Carry bit			Answer bit	Carry bit	Answer bit
A	B	C	D	E	F	C	F
0	0	0	1	0	0	0	0
0	1	0	1	1	1	0	1
1	0	0	1	1	1	0	1
1	1	1	0	1	0	1	0

Check: $0 + 0 = 0$
$0 + 1 = 1$
$1 + 0 = 1$
$1 + 1 = 10$

To perform useful arithmetic two half adders must be combined to give a *full adder* capable of handling the carry bits.

There are three main components of the CPU:

The Arithmetic and Logic Unit (ALU)
The Control Unit
The Memory (main store)

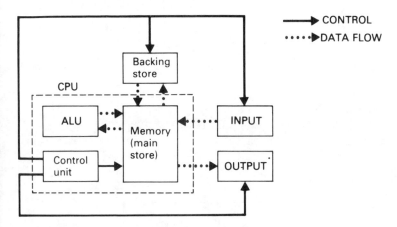

Fig. 6.7   *The Central Processing Unit and peripheral units*

Each of the three units (ALU, control unit, memory) contains *store locations* which may be 8–64 bits wide. Special store locations in the control unit and the ALU are known as *registers*. A register holds instructions and data which are currently being worked on or executed by the program. Program instructions are normally held in the main store and called up in turn to the register for execution. The process of calling up data and instructions from memory is carried out using data and control highways or buses. These are paths of wires typically 16 bits wide, which in practice are channels on printed circuit boards.

The clock
A computer requires a high speed flow of electrical pulses to be constantly available; a *quartz crystal* may be used to generate these pulses. A *clock* is used to regulate the speed of the pulses, e.g. 20 megahertz or 20 million pulses per second.

The memory
This is also known as the *main store* and the *Immediate Access Store (IAS)*.

Each store location may be 8–64 bits wide and contain *data* and *instructions*. The program differentiates between an instruction and a piece of data.

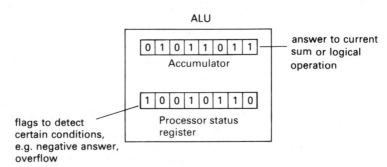

Fig. 6.8   *The memory. In practice, addresses may be 16–32 bits (2–4 bytes). Store locations may be 8–64 bits (1–8 bytes)*

The Arithmetic and Logic Unit (ALU)
This unit performs addition, subtraction and comparisons necessary in all types of processing.

ALU

| 0 | 1 | 0 | 1 | 1 | 0 | 1 | 1 |

Accumulator

answer to current sum or logical operation

| 1 | 0 | 0 | 1 | 0 | 1 | 1 | 0 |

Processor status register

flags to detect certain conditions, e.g. negative answer, overflow

Fig. 6.9   *The Arithmetic and Logic Unit*

The main register is the *accumulator* which holds the answer to the current operation. For example, if two numbers are to be added, a *copy* of the first is taken from memory and placed in the accumulator. The second number is then added to the first in the accumulator before the answer is returned to memory. Special instructions are available to perform these transfers between memory and accumulator.

A second register in the ALU, known as the *Processor Status Register (PSR)*, is used to monitor the results of the accumulator. The PSR can be checked by the program and corrective action taken if necessary, e.g. if an answer is too big, causing an overflow error.

The control unit

This unit contains two important registers, the *program counter* and the *instruction register*.

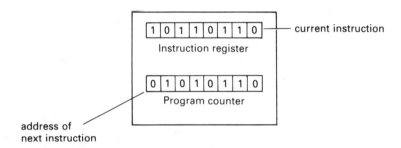

Fig. 6.10 *The Control Unit. The program counter contains an address which may be 16 or 32 bits wide in practice.*

The control unit is used to control the flow of instructions between the various components, i.e. memory, ALU and input and output units. This includes diverting bytes of data along the various data buses via a series of switches.

The program counter always holds the address in memory of the next instruction to be executed. This is fetched from memory and loaded into the instruction register. The program counter is incremented (increased by 1), in preparation for the next instruction. The instruction is executed. (Special instructions other than the user's program instructions, e.g. to open gates on data buses, are known as *micro instructions* and are stored as special microprograms on the computer's ROM chips.)

The process of fetching instructions from memory and then carrying them out is known as the *fetch–execute* cycle. Frequently this involves fetching characters and printing them on the screen by transferring them to a special area of the memory – the screen addresses. Or calculations may be performed by transferring numbers to the accumulator – the special register in the ALU capable of addition, subtraction, etc. The fetch–execute cycle is shown in detail on the next page.

KEY FACT

The *program counter* is an important register which holds the address of the next instruction to be fetched and executed. The program counter is part of the control unit.

The fetch–execute cycle

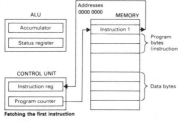

Fig. 6.11

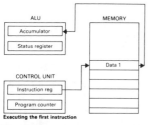

Fig. 6.12

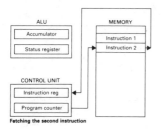

Fig. 6.13

Start

At start-up the program counter indicates the address of the first instruction.

Fetch

A *copy* of the first instruction is fetched from memory and placed in the instruction register.

Simultaneously, the program counter is incremented (increased by 1) to point to the address of the next instruction.

Execute

The instruction in the instruction register is executed. In this example a byte of data is copied from memory into the accumulator.

N.B. Copying data or instructions from memory into the registers leaves the contents of the memory unchanged.

Fetch

A copy of the next instruction is fetched from memory and placed in the instruction register. (The previous instruction is *overwritten.*) Simultaneously, the program counter is incremented to give the address of the next instruction.

The cycle continues until a branch or jump instruction occurs as described in the next section.

KEY FACTS

Each instruction would typically consist of an 8-bit instruction code and a 16-bit operand. The operand could be an address in the memory.

| 8-bit opcode | 16-bit operand |

| 1 | 0 | 1 | 0 | 1 | 1 | 0 | 1 | 0 | 1 | 0 | 1 | 1 | 0 | 1 | 1 | 0 | 1 | 1 | 0 | 1 | 1 | 0 | 1 |

instruction   address

Typical meaning: 'Load the accumulator with the byte(s) contained at the following address'.

Each type of processor has a finite set of instructions. These are available directly to the programmer using *hexadecimal machine code* or *assembly language*. A particular computer might have 70–100 instructions available.

Some of the latest very powerful microcomputers are known as *RISC machines (Reduced Instruction Set Computers)*. These restrict the instruction set to a few most frequently used ones, and construct the others when needed. This enables the computer to run much faster, e.g. 10 mips (millions of instructions per second).

The following table shows a few examples from a complete instruction set of perhaps 80 instructions. Each instruction is shown in binary, hexadecimal and assembly language (mnemonic) form.

Description	Binary		Hexadecimal	Mnemonic
Load the accumulator	1010	1101	AD	LDA
Add a number to the contents of the accumulator	0110	1101	6D	ADC
Store the contents of the accumulator (at a certain address)	1000	1101	8D	STA

Branching

The fetch–execute cycle continues through all the instructions in the program, executing the instructions in sequence as the program counter is incremented. This routine is broken if the programmer specifies a *branch* or *jump* to another instruction at an address which is not part of the incremental sequence.

Instead of the program counter being incremented, the programmer may place a new address in the program counter. This causes the program to jump or branch out of sequence.

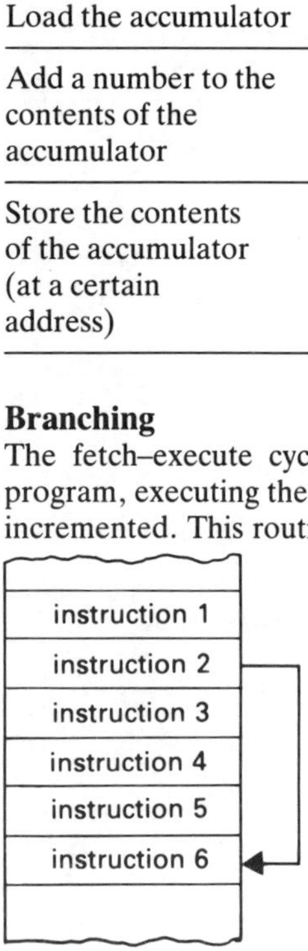

After instruction 2 has been executed, the program jumps to instruction 6, missing out instructions 3–5.

Fig. 6.14

Unconditional branch

If the branch takes place automatically, this is known as an *unconditional branch* or *unconditional jump*, e.g. JMP is the assembly language command to jump to a new address. JMP corresponds to the much-criticised GOTO statement in BASIC. Similarly JSR (jump to sub-routine) corresponds to GOSUB and PROC – which are unconditional branches to sub-routines/procedures in BASIC.

Conditional branch

In a *conditional branch* or *jump*, the branch only takes place if a certain condition is true during execution of the program; for example, if the result of an addition is negative. This could be tested for by the *processor status register* in the ALU. If a negative answer results, the negative flag is set (to 1) and the program detects this. The result would be a branch in the program.

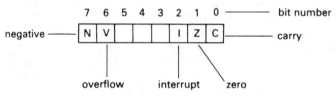

Fig. 6.15   *The Processor Status Register*

Some of the main bits of a processor status register are shown in the diagram. The bits contain 1 or 0 to indicate the presence or absence of certain conditions in the accumulator. The program tests these bits after addition, etc., enabling a branch to be either made or not made.

Typical conditional branch instructions are:

Assembly language instruction	Meaning
BVC	Branch if overflow flag is 0
BMI	Branch if result of previous sum was minus
BEQ	Branch if result of previous sum was 0

For example: BNE ALPHA (Branch if not equal to zero, to ALPHA)

where ALPHA is a *label* representing the destination after branching. Labels such as ALPHA are arbitrary names made up by the programmer; they correspond to line numbers in a BASIC program.

The conditional branch may be used in an assembly language routine, for example to repeat a process a certain number of times.

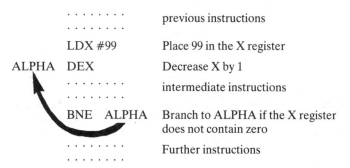

	. . . .	previous instructions
	LDX #99	Place 99 in the X register
ALPHA	DEX	Decrease X by 1
	. . . .	intermediate instructions
	BNE ALPHA	Branch to ALPHA if the X register does not contain zero
	. . . .	Further instructions

The LDX instruction places the number 99 in the *X register*; this is a special register in the ALU, which can be incremented (increased by 1) or decremented (decreased by 1). After the X register has been decremented, BNE checks to see if its contents are zero; if not the program branches back to the label ALPHA. This is an example of a *loop*, where a section of a program is repeated a number of times. In this example the loop would be repeated 100 times (until the X register contains zero). In BASIC and some other high level languages, conditional branches may be generated by IF . . . THEN . . . , REPEAT . . . UNTIL . . . , DO . . . WHILE . . . , etc.

Interrupt
The execution of a program may stop temporarily to allow some activity involving peripheral devices; for example, if data has to be copied from the memory to a printer. This is known as a *program interrupt*.

Execution of the program resumes at the point reached before the interrupt. The processor status register holds the necessary flags to enable the program to continue at the point where it was interrupted.

Breakpoint
An instruction may be inserted in a program to stop the program and allow the programmer to examine various registers and variables; this may be for 'debugging' purposes or program development. After the *breakpoint instruction* has been executed and the registers examined, modifications may be made to the program. The processor then returns to the main program to execute the next instruction following the point at which the break occurred.

1 Name the three parts of the central processing unit (CPU).
(NISEC Specimen Paper II, Section A, Qu. 1)

2 (a) State *one* difference between a register in the CPU and a location in main memory.
  (b) Describe the purpose of the program counter.
  (c) Describe the purpose of the instruction register.
(LEAG Specimen Paper 3, Qu. 13)

3 What happens during the fetch part of the fetch–execute cycle?
(LEAG Specimen Paper 3, Qu. 14)

4 Three parts of the CPU of a computer are given below. Explain the function of each part.
  (a) Control unit.
  (b) Logical processing unit.
  (c) Main storage.
(NEA Specimen Paper 1, Qu. 5)

5

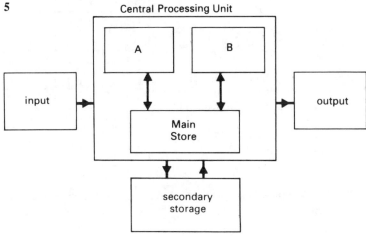

Fig. 6.16

Name the parts A and B in the Central Processing Unit part of the diagram.
(WJEC Specimen Paper 1, Qu. 3(a))

6 A central heating system has a boiler. If it is COLD and the clock is ON, the boiler is switched ON. In all other cases the boiler is switched OFF.

Complete the truth table to show when the boiler is ON and when it is OFF.

Input		Output
Temp.	*Clock*	*Boiler*
COLD	OFF	
COLD	ON	
HOT	OFF	
HOT	ON	

(MEG Specimen Paper 1, Section F, Qu. 9)

7 A water pump for a room heating system is to switch on if all the following conditions are fulfilled:

1 The room is cold.
2 Hot water is available.
3 It is during the time set on the time switch or the manual override switch is set to 'on'.

Complete the section of truth table shown alongside for this situation using the codes:

R = 1 means room warm enough;
W = 1 means hot water is available;
T = 1 means set time for heating to be on;
M = 1 means manual override switch is set to 'on';
P = 1 means pump on.

Inputs				Output
R	W	T	M	P
0	0	1	0	
0	0	1	1	
0	1	0	0	
0	1	0	1	
0	1	1	0	
0	1	1	1	
1	0	1	1	
1	1	0	0	
1	1	1	0	
1	1	1	1	

(NEA Specimen Paper 1, Qu. 4)

8 Fill in each of the blank spaces in the table with 0 or 1 as appropriate, to represent the outputs P, Q and R for the given logic network.

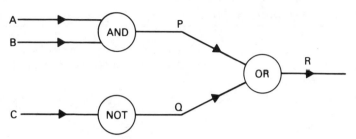

Fig. 6.17

A	B	C	P	Q	R
0	0	0	0	1	1
0	0	1	0	0	
0	1	0	0		
0	1	1	0		
1	0	0			
1	0	1			
1	1	0			
1	1	1			

(MEG Specimen Paper 2, Section B, Qu. 11)

In order to perform useful work the computer must be programmed. A *program* is a set of instructions which do simple tasks at high speed; these might include:

- calculations
- sorting
- drawing pictures
- producing sound
- controlling machinery

As described in the previous section, the instructions are stored, alongside any data, as bytes (sets of bits or binary digits 0,1) in the computer's memory.

opcode	operand

| 1 | 0 | 1 | 0 | 1 | 1 | 0 | 1 | 0 | 1 | 0 | 1 | 1 | 0 | 1 | 1 | 0 | 1 | 1 | 0 | 1 | 1 | 0 | 1 |

instruction   address

Computer programmer

When a computer program is first written it is usually planned on paper as a set of *modules* or *procedures*. These are blocks of program instructions which perform separate tasks, e.g. to draw a circle. Several different people could each develop a module before assembling all the separate modules into a complete package. The process of developing a large program might take several months or even years.

Computer user

A fully developed program would normally be stored on disk or ROM chip; this could be supplied, together with suitable training and instruction manuals, to a *computer user*, to help with his or her particular job.

KEY FACTS

The difference between a programmer and a computer user should be clearly understood.

Programmer: A person who writes, develops and maintains computer programs.

Computer user: A person who may not be a computing expert, but who uses a computer to help with their work, e.g. doctor, policeman, secretary, musician, artist.

Machine code

The binary digits used in the machine's own language or instruction set are normally called *machine code*. This is the lowest level of computer language. To save writing and remembering long sets of bits, the machine code programmer represents every four bits by a single *hexadecimal* character.

Binary		1 0 1 0		1 0 0 1
Hexadecimal		A		9

Advantages of machine code

- It is the machine's own language and doesn't need *translating*.
- It gives precise control over the various parts of the computer, e.g. memory locations, *interfacing* to external devices (robots, etc.)
- Programs run very fast.

Disadvantages

- Machine code is very difficult to learn/remember.
- Machine code programs are very hard to modify.

Assembly languages (or low level languages)

True binary or hexadecimal machine codes are very difficult for programming since the codes give no indication of their meaning. For example, 1 0 1 0 1 0 0 1 does not suggest 'Load the Accumulator'. In assembly language, a single instruction is represented by a *mnemonic*. A mnemonic is an aid to the human memory; for example 'Load the Accumulator' is LDA in assembly language mnemonic form.

mnemonics
STA:	Store the contents of the accumulator
ADC:	Add with carry
JMP:	Jump
BNE:	Branch if negative
INX:	Increment a special register

Assembly language instructions (mnemonics)

A program written in assembly language must be translated into true binary machine code using an *assembler*; an assembler is itself a program. Assembly language is often referred to as *low level language*.

Advantages of assembly language

- It is easier for humans to understand than machine code.
- One assembly language instruction corresponds exactly to one machine code instruction (binary) – it is therefore relatively easy to translate.
- Programs written in assembly language are fast in execution.
- The programmer has precise control over the parts of the computer.

Disadvantages

- Assembly languages are not the same for different types of computer so programs may not easily be transferred between makes – lack of 'portability'.
- Assembly languages are not very 'user-friendly' (although easier than machine code).

Uses of assembly language

The experienced programmer may include small procedures or 'mini-programs' within a large program. These might include a sort routine or a screen dump. Such routines might need high speed or precise control of devices such as the printer. To achieve this speed or control, the sub-routines may be written in assembly language, but incorporated in the large program written in a high level language such as BASIC. Assembly language may also be used to write *utility programs* or *systems software* needed for the operation of a computer, e.g. the *compilers* (programs which translate high level languages into machine code). Complex drawing or games programs may also require the speed and accuracy of assembly language. Three instructions in assembly language are shown below:

	Operation code	Operand
Instruction 1	LDA	#37
Instruction 2	ADC	62337
Instruction 3	STA	62338

The above assembly language routine can be translated as follows:

- Load the accumulator with the decimal number 37.
- Add the number stored at address 62337 (decimal) to the number stored in the accumulator (37).
- Store the number in the accumulator (the answer to the addition) at memory location 62338.

High level languages

Farthest away from the computer's own (binary) machine code, the high level languages use complete words taken from the English language. They are therefore relatively easy to learn and accessible to a much wider audience than the low level languages and machine code. The high level languages have names such as COBOL, FORTRAN, Pascal, BASIC, Logo and C, and are intended to be easy for humans to learn and remember. Many of the languages share common words such as PRINT, REPEAT . . . UNTIL, IF . . . THEN . . . , READ . . . , DO . . . LOOP, WHILE . . . DO, CASE . . . OF.

The relative friendliness of the high level languages is obtained at the expense of efficiency in the execution of programs. This is because each keyword, such as PRINT, must be *translated* into machine code. PRINT, for example, actually translates into a small set of machine code instructions, known as a sub-routine or *microprogram*.

The process of translation may be performed in one of two ways:

- by a *compiler*,
- by an *interpreter*.

Compilers and interpreters are computer programs; they form part of the systems software.

The compiler
The compiler takes the *complete program* in a high level language and

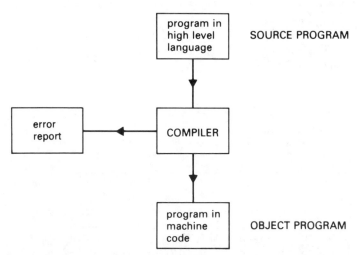

Fig. 7.1 *The compiler produces a complete machine code program which can be stored on disk and run independently*

translates this in its entirety into machine code. Any errors in compiling are reported. The resulting machine code may be permanently saved on disk and run in the future *ad infinitum*. The compiler is itself a complex program and may be too large for use on the smaller microcomputers (in this case an *interpreter* is used). One disadvantage is that compiled programs are difficult to edit.

The interpreter
The interpreter is a simpler program than the compiler and is used on microcomputers with smaller memories. The interpreter results in slower program execution than the compiler.

Uses of high level languages
High level languages are *applications* based; some languages are suitable for scientific or *mathematical* work, while others may be directed towards *file handling* or *education*. There are often many different 'dialects' of the same language, e.g. BASIC; this prevents *portability* of programs between different brands of computer.

Attempts to improve portability have been made by establishing international standard versions of a language, e.g. ISO Pascal.

Advantages of high level languages
As they are close to English, high level language programs are:

● relatively easy to understand;
● easy to modify;
● portable between different computers (if standard 'dialects' of the language are used).

Disadvantages

● Programs must be translated to machine code, which may be a slow process.
● High level programs do not give precise control over the components of the computer. Assembly language is more accurate.

KEY FACTS
Compilers and interpreters are *programs* and form part of the *systems software* of the computer. These *translation* programs may be supplied with a computer on built-in ROM chips; alternatively the programs may be supplied on disk. This enables a computer to run programs written in different languages, for example, Pascal, BASIC or C.

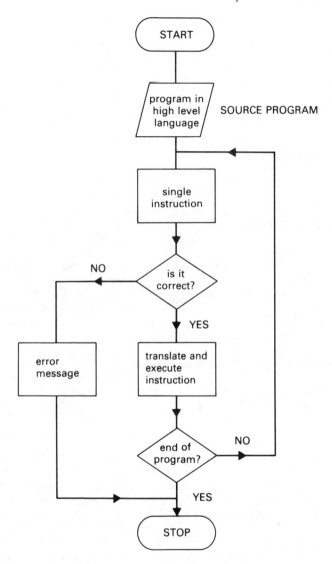

Fig. 7.2 *The interpreter. Each instruction must be translated every time it is executed. There is no complete object program in machine code*

Examples of high level languages

BASIC: Beginners All-Purpose Symbolic Instruction Code

This was designed as an educational language and is standard on many microcomputers. The main criticism is that there are many different dialects, preventing portability between computers. BASIC programs are also criticised for their lack of *structure*, i.e. the program is not divided into a series of meaningful blocks each with a clear purpose. BBC BASIC is regarded as one of the better versions since programs may be written as a set of procedures: *modular* or *structured* programming is encouraged.

The educational language COMAL includes many of the features of BASIC within a more structured framework.

Microcomputers usually have a systems program known as an *editor* to enable mistakes in programs to be corrected on the screen. Languages such as BASIC and COMAL, residing in small microcomputers, are usually *interpreted* rather than *compiled* – so execution is relatively slow.

Pascal

Pascal is a general-purpose language which encourages good structure. As there are no line numbers, programs must be written in separate modules or procedures. An international standard, ISO Pascal, ensures portability between different machines. Pascal is a *compiled* language so execution of programs is fast. Pascal is used in colleges and universities and by professional programmers writing commercial software.

COBOL: Common Business-Orientated Language

This is one of the oldest languages and uses statements very similar to English sentences. It is intended primarily for handling very large files of data and is used on mainframe computers, e.g. in banks, building societies, large commercial/industrial organisations.

FORTRAN: Formula Translation

FORTRAN is a high level language used for mathematical work in science and engineering, e.g. aircraft design. FORTRAN was one of the first languages used on mainframe computers, and as it is compiled, is also used on powerful microcomputers. Being biased towards mathematics, FORTRAN is weak in text file handling.

Logo

This language is derived from the language LISP (List Processing). Logo is widely used with young children, for drawing (turtle graphics) and controlling small robotic vehicles. Procedures can be assembled from simple commands. Logotron Logo is a popular version of the language used in schools; for example:

```
TO TWOSQUARES:    steps
   SQUARE:        steps LT 90 PENUP
   FORWARD:       steps PENDOWN
   SQUARE:        steps/2
   END
```

Computer languages summary

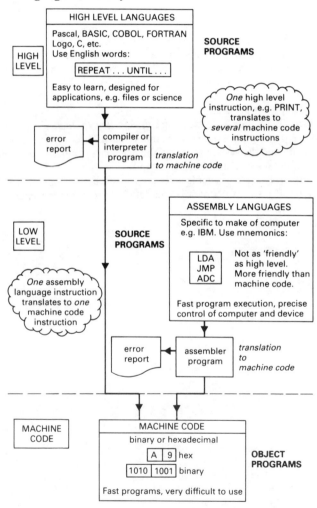

Fig. 7.3

FORTH

This is a high level language which possesses all the speed and precision of low level languages. It is used for controlling machinery, e.g. washing machines, large telescopes, and for writing compilers and computer games.

A distinguishing feature of FORTH is that new commands may be continually defined by the user and added to a dictionary – FORTH is not a finite list of commands.

C

This is one of the newer high level languages and is increasingly popular. Programmers in C are in demand, as the language is closely associated with the network operating system UNIX – which was written in C. C is also used for writing systems software such as compilers.

4GLs/program generators

Fourth Generation languages or *software development tools* simplify the writing of programs. The programmer specifies requirements such as the data files and the system *generates* the necessary *programming code*, taking care of details such as the screen layout.

Authoring systems enable software for teaching/training purposes to be generated easily by people without detailed programming skills.

Modular or structured programming

Most commercial programs are written in one of the high level languages, such as FORTRAN, COBOL or Pascal. It is normal to plan the overall program in a very rough outline first, i.e. as a series of *blocks* or *modules* each representing a different *task*. These modules are known as *sub-routines* or *procedures*. The procedures are often called up from a *menu* or choice of options; a procedure can therefore be executed as often as required during the execution of a program. The procedure is a small independent program within a main program.

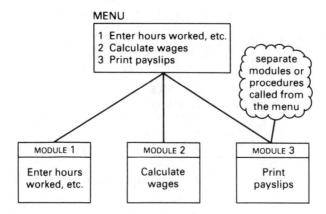

Fig. 7.4 *Procedures for a menu-driven program*

The simplified diagram shows the outline plan for a wages program. A program which is composed of a series of procedures or sub-routines is called a *structured program*. An unstructured program consists of a large number of *branches* (e.g. GOTO statements) with no clearly defined sections.

The method of designing a program by first defining a set of procedures is known as the *top-down method*. At this stage of the design no programming instructions have been written; the coding in a high level language is done later.

Advantages of structured programs

● Several programmers can produce different procedures for the same program.

- Structured programs are easier to understand. This is important when someone has to modify or maintain a program written by another programmer.
- Procedures or sub-routines can be easily fitted into new programs; a library of useful routines can be accumulated, saving programming time.

Algorithm

In planning a program module or procedure, it may be necessary to plan a complex operation as a series of logical steps. The list of steps needed to solve a problem is sometimes called an *algorithm*. Alternatively, the algorithm might be presented in the form of a *flowchart*. An algorithm to find the average of a set of numbers could be described as follows.

```
Set total and counter to 0
Repeat
        Read a number
        Add it to total
        Add one to counter
Until the end of the data
Calculate the average
Print average
```

Algorithm described in statements

The algorithm might also be described as a flowchart: see Figure 7.5 opposite.

After the algorithm has been defined as a list of statements or as a flowchart, it is coded in a high level language.

```
 10    total = 0
 20    counter = 0
 30    REPEAT
 40            INPUT number
 50            IF number = −999 THEN 80
 60            total = total + number
 70            counter = counter + 1
 80    UNTIL   number = −999
 90    average = total/counter
100    PRINT average
```

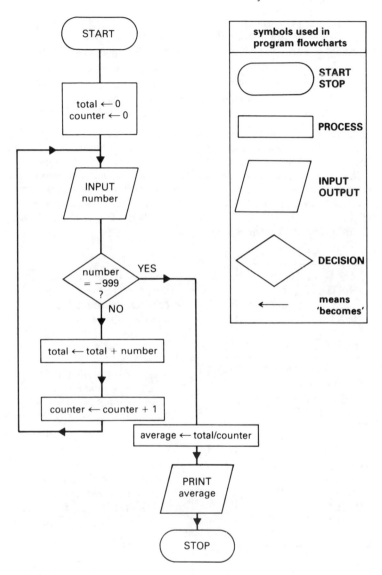

Fig. 7.5 *Program flowchart*

Programming constructs

In the small program example written in BBC BASIC, a number of important constructs common to most high level languages are shown:

e.g.	REPEAT	The statements between REPEAT . . .
	. . . . . .	UNTIL . . . are executed until
	. . . . . .	something is true – in this case
	UNTIL	till the number −999 is entered.

−999 is a *rogue value* or *dummy data* used to mark the end of the genuine numbers. In *alphabetic* data ZZZ or *** might be used. The IF . . . THEN . . . statement is used to branch to another part of the program.

There are many other constructs in high level languages normally used for repetition or branching. These occur in structured languages such as Pascal, COMAL, FORTRAN and BBC BASIC. The constructs FOR . . . NEXT . . . , REPEAT . . . UNTIL . . . , WHILE . . . DO all cause repetition and are known as *loops*.

FOR . . . NEXT . . .

```
FOR N = 1 TO 10
INPUT number
total = total + number
NEXT N
```

The loop is used to repeat the process a fixed number of times, i.e. to read and total 10 numbers.

WHILE . . . DO

```
WHILE number <> −999 DO
READ number
total = total + number
END WHILE
```

The loop is repeated while a certain condition is true (number is not equal to −999)

CASE . . . OF . . .

```
CASE number OF
WHEN >0
PRINT 'POSITIVE'
WHEN <0
PRINT 'NEGATIVE'
END CASE
```

CASE is used with a list of alternatives, instead of IF . . . THEN . . .

Variables

The store locations in a computer's memory, although existing as binary addresses in RAM, are given names by the programmer. These are usually meaningful *labels*. For example, in a file of library books the names of the store locations might be:

variable	*description*
title	: the title of the book
author	: the author's name
isbn	: the International Standard Book Number
category	: the classification of book

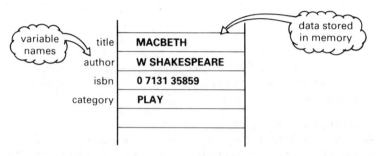

Fig. 7.6

Since there will be thousands of books in a library, there will be very many different contents of each store – the data in each store is *variable*. One store location, e.g. *author*, can only hold one set of data at a given time. If *author* contains the name DICKENS, it must be *overwritten* if it is to contain SHAKESPEARE.

An *array* enables the same variable name to hold several thousand pieces of similar data, within the limits of the computer's memory. This is done by attaching a *subscript* to the end of each variable.

variable	*contents of store location*	
author(1)	DICKENS	
author(2)	SHAKESPEARE	
author(3)	KEATS	*variable name*: author
author(4)	CHAUCER	
author(5)	AUSTEN	
author(6)	BRONTE	

A one-dimensional array

Two-dimensional array

Tables of figures or *matrices* consisting of rows and columns may form a *two-dimensional* array, for example:

	column 1	*column 2*
	MONO SCREEN £	COLOUR SCREEN £
row 1 ACE MICRO	499	649
row 2 ZODIAC	349	499
row 3 ELITE	409	542

price (3,2)
(row 3, column 2)

Arrays are normally *declared* or *dimensioned* at the start of a program; this announces the number of elements that the memory will need to hold, e.g. DIM price (100).

Local and global variables

A variable may have a certain value in one part of a program, normally in a procedure or sub-routine; if this value does not continue throughout the whole program, the variable is said to be *local*.

In the following example, a *procedure* is used to read five numbers. The numbers are indexed using a variable called *counter*. *Counter* is a local variable within the procedure enclosed by DEF PROCread . . . ENDPROC.

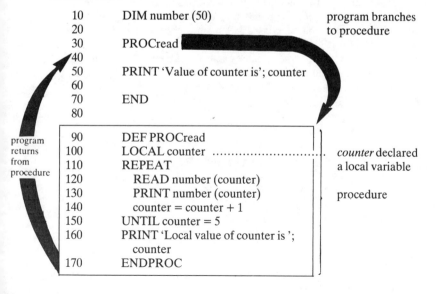

```
10      DIM number (50)                          program branches
20                                                to procedure
30      PROCread
40
50      PRINT 'Value of counter is'; counter
60
70      END
80

90      DEF PROCread
100     LOCAL counter .........................  counter declared
110     REPEAT                                    a local variable
120        READ number (counter)
130        PRINT number (counter)                 procedure
140        counter = counter + 1
150     UNTIL counter = 5
160     PRINT 'Local value of counter is ';
           counter
170     ENDPROC
```

program returns from procedure

```
180
190   DATA 9,4,8,9,6,4,3,2,9,8,4,5
```

Program listing

```
              9
              4
              8
              9
              6
Local value of counter is 5
  Value of counter is 0
```

Output when the program is run

As shown by the program output, just before leaving the procedure (line 160), the value of *counter* has risen to 5. After leaving the procedure (line 50) the value of *counter* has returned to its default value of 0.

A *global variable* has the same value throughout an entire program and its various procedures/sub-routines.

Testing and debugging

The dry run

This is a test of a program or an algorithm carried out *manually*, i.e. using paper and pencil. The dry run tests the *logic* of the program. In testing a wages program, for example, a dry run would involve calculating a sample wage slip by hand. This could be compared with a computer calculation on the same data, thereby testing the correctness of the program.

A dry run on the averages program given previously would be:

DATA 5,9,6,8,-999

Variables	1st pass	2nd pass	3rd pass	4th pass	5th pass	
number	5	9	6	8	-999	
total	5	14	20	28	28	program branches
counter	1	2	3	4	4	to calculate the average
average	0	0	0	0	28/4=7	

Debugging

Before a program can be used it must be thoroughly tested under all operating conditions. At various stages of development, errors may become apparent. The process of testing and correcting errors in a program is known as *debugging*.

Syntax errors (or compilation errors)

These are mistakes in the use of the program's language, such as:

- PLINT instead of PRINT
- missing or odd number of brackets.

Syntax errors are reported by the *compiler* or *interpreter* and must be corrected using an *editor* before the program can be successfully run or executed.

Logical errors

These result from a mistake in the *design* of a program, such as branching to the wrong line number or performing a subtraction in the wrong order. This may not cause the program to stop, but the answer will not be correct.

Execution errors

An execution error or *run-time* error causes the program to stop during running and an error message appears on the screen or on printout. Examples might be an attempt to divide by zero or a calculation which produces an answer too big for the computer (overflow).

Program listings and traces

The *listing* is a printout on paper of the entire set of instructions which make up a program and is essential at various stages in the development of a large program.

The *trace* is a printout or screen display of the values of all of the variables leading up to an error. This enables the programmer to identify the exact location of an error.

Program documentation

This is a complete description of a program intended to enable other programmers to understand and modify it (*program maintenance*). It is essential when one programmer leaves and a new programmer continues to develop the program.

Program documentation might include:

- a list of variables and descriptions
- a program listing
- a flowchart

- sample input data and output
- descriptions of modules or procedures, with explanations

Software is the programs used to run a computer, usually stored on disk or ROM chip. There are two main categories of software:

Systems software: essential for the operation and control of the computer (whatever the task).

Applications packages: used for a particular task in business, industry, education, e.g. wordprocessing.

Systems software
Systems software is normally supplied as part of a new computer and may be stored internally on ROM chips or externally on floppy disks. Some of the main systems programs are:

- translation programs
- operating systems
- utility programs

Translation programs
Assemblers are programs used for translating other programs in *assembly (low level) languages*, into *machine code*. *Compilers* and *interpreters* are used to translate *high level languages* into machine code. These programs were discussed in the previous section.

Operating systems
All computers need programs to control the various peripheral devices (printers, etc.) and to supervise the loading and saving of files using disks. These functions are carried out by one or more programs known as the *operating system*. The computer user communicates with the operating system by entering commands in immediate mode, such as RUN, SAVE, PRINT, etc. The operating system may respond by reporting error messages on the screen or operator's console. The operating system, being a program, must be loaded into memory itself; this is often done automatically by another small program in ROM called a *bootstrap*.

On microcomputers the operating system CP/M (control program for microprocessors) was dominant for several years; this has been superseded by MSDOS (Microsoft Disk Operating System) on IBM and IBM-compatible business machines. The need to learn many obscure operating system commands is being reduced by the arrival of 'user-friendly' 'front ends'. These mask the operating system by enabling all commands to be executed using a mouse and pointer.

Minicomputers often use an operating system known as UNIX. This is designed for use with *networks* of computers and is also becoming more popular with the advent of very powerful 32-bit microcomputers. Networks which allow many different users to access a central computer are known as *multi-access systems*. Users a long distance away from the computer may make input and output using *remote terminals*.

Multiprogramming or *multitasking* is the running of several programs apparently at the same time; in fact the processor alternates between programs while one program is held up by one of the slower peripheral devices such as the printer. (The processor operates very much faster than the electro-mechanical devices such as the printer.)

Utility programs

These are systems programs often needed for routine 'housekeeping' tasks. Typical utility programs are used to:

- prepare (*format*) a new disk with *tracks* and *sectors*
- copy files from one disk to another
- copy a graphics screen onto paper (screen 'dump')
- carry out *sorting* (into alphabetical or numerical order)
- check spelling in a wordprocessing document

Applications programs

Applications programs are designed to increase efficiency in offices and factories, etc. The programs may be operated by computer users who are not computing experts. Typical applications programs would be:

- wordprocessors
- spreadsheets
- databases
- communications (Electronic Mail, Videotex)
- payroll
- accountancy/stock control
- theatre booking
- desktop publishing
- CAD/CAM, graphics

An applications program might be written to solve a specific problem in a particular firm. This is known as *bespoke software* since it is 'tailored' to the needs of the firm concerned.

Applications packages

A large amount of applications software is available 'off the shelf' in the form of standard applications packages. An applications package consists of:

- programs on disk or ROM chip
- user instructions (handbook)
- training courses (perhaps)

Many applications packages for microcomputers have sold in very large numbers throughout the world, for example:

Name of package	*Application*
Wordstar and Word Perfect	wordprocessing
SuperCalc and Lotus 1-2-3	spreadsheets/financial planning
dBase II and dBase III	database (filing) systems

User documentation
The user of an applications package is very often not a computing expert. Typical computer users might be:

shopkeeper	garage owner/mechanic	doctor
secretary	policeman/woman	farmer
accountant	teacher	engineer/scientist
bank employee	author/journalist	weather forecaster

It is, therefore, important that the instruction/operating manual provides all the support needed to run the software. User documentation, which is *non-technical*, should include:

- instructions to load and run the program
- details of the required input (format of data) and expected output
- advice on the correction of common errors
- instructions on the setting up of a printer (configuration)
- perhaps a telephone 'hotline' for help

The user documentation would *not* contain:

1. Program listings 2. Lists of variables 3. Program flowcharts.

KEY FACTS

Program documentation:	The technical details of a program, listings, etc., intended for other programmers
User documentation:	An instruction manual which should enable a *non-expert* user to use fully all the facilities of the program

---

Examples of applications packages in the electronic office
The 'electronic office' relies on the use of standard *applications packages*. Some people refer to the 'paperless' office although it is unlikely that paper will ever disappear – computers use paper as their main medium for permanent output or 'hard copy'.

The main applications packages in the electronic office are:

- the wordprocessor
- the spreadsheet

- the database
- communications (Electronic Mail), fax (facsimile machines)

The database and communications packages are discussed in detail in separate chapters of this book; graphics and design/desktop publishing packages are used in specialised offices in fields such as advertising and architecture. The wordprocessor and spreadsheet are found in most businesses and their basic functions are as follows.

Wordprocessing
This is probably the most popular applications package for micro-computers. Some of the main features of the wordprocessor are described here.

Text can be *edited* before it is printed on paper – correcting fluid becomes obsolete. Some of these editing facilities are very powerful.

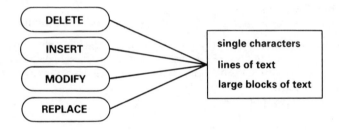

Fig. 7.7

Any large block of text can be *moved* to another position within a document (equivalent to the 'cut and paste' operation using scissors and glue). The width of left and right *margins* may be set and reset many times throughout a report.

The text may be *justified* (vertically aligned down the right-hand or left-hand side).

Text can be filed on disk and *retrieved* later, perhaps being modified before printing. A first draft might be printed on paper using double line-spacing: this is then submitted to the originator and the script is corrected by hand. The changes can then be inserted in the wordprocessor version without retyping the entire document. The final edition of the document is then printed. The user may specify single line-spacing for the final copy by a simple command entered at the keyboard (and perhaps change from *dot-matrix* to *daisywheel* printer).

The standard letter

A standard letter can be typed once but sent to many different individuals by *infilling* their personal details automatically from a file. Infilling consists of inserting individual details into marked spaces left in the standard letter. *Multiple copies* may be made.

Wordprocessors are frequently used by:

- secretaries and typists
- journalists and authors
- students and researchers

The spreadsheet

This is a popular type of program used for the processing of *numerical tables*. These tables (or 'matrices') are frequently used in accountancy where they are known as spreadsheets, but the program may be used whenever tables of figures are to be calculated, e.g. football league tables.

The use of a spreadsheet involves two basic elements:

- the computer program or software
- the spreadsheet itself, created by the user

The program is used to create a spreadsheet by entering the tabular data at the keyboard and this is saved on disk as a *file* or collection of data. The file is quite separate from the program used to create it, though they may reside on the same disk.

A very simple spreadsheet is shown below.

	A	B	C	D	E
1	ITEM	NO	UNIT COST	TOTAL COST	VAT
2			£	£	£
3	shoes	12	9.97	119.64	17.95
4	shirts	15	13.53	202.95	30.44
5	gloves	13	5.97	77.61	11.64
6	ties	26	5.32	138.32	20.75
7	scarves	28	3.86	108.08	16.21

cell E4

The cell may contain words, numbers or formulae – e.g. to calculate VAT or add a column of figures.

Fig. 7.8 *A simple spreadsheet*

The spreadsheet file may be retrieved from disk for further use or modification and a simple command enables the sheet to be printed on paper. One program therefore enables many different spreadsheets to be created and filed separately on disk.

A practical spreadsheet might extend to several thousand rows and columns. Each column would be several characters wide as specified by the user.

Recalculation – What if?

A very important feature of the spreadsheet is that cells can contain *formulae*, e.g. to calculate VAT or to multiply two cells together, e.g. B3*C3. If a figure is altered somewhere in the spreadsheet, the whole spreadsheet is *recalculated automatically*. This makes the spreadsheet very useful as a management tool for making predictions about the future. These are known as '*what if*' speculations:

- What if prices rose by 10%?
- What if VAT increased to 20%?

The user simply enters the new percentage in the appropriate cell and the whole spreadsheet is recalculated almost instantly.

The spreadsheet is most useful to managers, accountants, scientists and engineers needing to calculate (and recalculate) large tables of figures. It saves hours of working compared with pencil and paper.

Expert systems and artificial intelligence (AI)

The *expert system* is a software package which attempts to emulate the human expert who possesses vast knowledge and 'rule of thumb' methods based on years of experience. This work is progressing in fields such as medicine, geological exploration and insurance risk assessment. In theory, it should be possible to create a massive *archive* representing most of the experience of, say, several eminent medical consultants. Providing that suitable routines for *cross-referencing*, interrogating, and drawing conclusions can be programmed, such expertise can be made available very quickly to a much wider audience.

A *shell* is a program used to create an expert system on any subject. Its name is derived from the fact that it is supplied empty of data or 'content free'.

Critics of artificial intelligence suggest that a computer will never accurately copy human thought since the machine has no soul. However, research has shown that the diagnosis of physical illnesses can be greatly improved by the use of a computer system to assist the doctor; newly qualified doctors using expert systems can increase their diagnostic success rate to the level of experienced consultants. It is claimed that the computer, unlike the human, always asks the right questions and does not overlook important evidence.

Two of the main programming languages used in artificial intelligence work are LISP and PROLOG: these work on *knowledge bases* which contain not only *data*, but also *relationships* between pieces of data.

1 Choose one item from the given list to complete the sentence.

   starting value   control value
   rogue value   counter
   check digit

   A value which can mark the end of the data is called a . . . .
   (MEG Specimen Paper 1, Section G, Qu. 2)

2 Computer programs can be written using 'high level' or 'low level'
   languages.
   (*a*) Give *one* advantage of using a 'high level' language.
   (*b*) Give *one* advantage of using a 'low level' language.
   (LEAG Specimen Paper 1, Qu. 19)

3 Computers can now be programmed in a variety of high level languages. Explain the benefits of this variety of high level languages.
   (NEA Specimen Paper 1, Qu. 10)

4 Utility programs and applications programs are two types of software.
   Tick the one which is an *applications* program.

   A program to format the tracks
   and sectors on a magnetic
   disk   . . . .

   A program to carry out stock
   control   . . . .

   A program to transfer data from
   magnetic disk to magnetic
   tape   . . . .
   (SEG Specimen Paper 2, Qu. 2)

5 A computer program written in a high level language needs to be
   translated before execution. Which of the following describes this
   process?

   A Object code → compiler → source code
   B Object code → interpreter → source code
   C Source code → assembler → object code
   D Source code → compiler → object code
   (SEG Summer 1988 Paper 1, Qu. 40)

6 A newsagent buys a microcomputer to help with her business. One of
   the 'utility programs' provided allows her to make copies of her disks.
   Describe two more utility programs that she might use.

The newsagent buys an 'applications package' to help with the customer accounts. Describe another package which might prove useful.

(LEAG Specimen Paper 1, Qu. 18)

7 In a particular application the source code was written in a high level language. This was translated by a computer into object code. What is the name of the program which translated the source code into object code?

(MEG Specimen Paper 2, Section C, Qu. 14)

8 Computers are usually supplied with software called compilers, interpreters or assemblers.

(*a*) What is meant by software?
(*b*) What is the purpose of such software?
(*c*) What distinguishes an interpreter from a compiler?
(*d*) What distinguishes assemblers from compilers and interpreters?

(NEA Specimen Paper 1, Qu. 8)

9 The technique of checking the logic of a program by inserting additional statements to print out variable values is called

A dry running   **C** tracing
B verifying   **D** compiling

(SEG Specimen Paper 1, Qu. 4)

10 Give one example of a utility program and two examples of applications packages.

(MEG Specimen Paper 1, Section F, Qu. 14)

At its simplest level, a *file* can be thought of as a set of records written manually on cards.

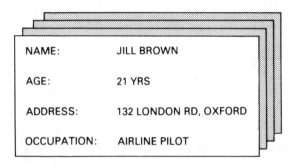

Fig. 8.1

The computer file has many advantages over the manual paper or *card index* system.

Computer files:

- take up less room than cards
- can be *updated* (changed) more easily
- enable particular records to be found more quickly (*searching* or *information retrieval*)
- can be automatically *sorted* into a particular order

Databases

A collection of files stored on magnetic disk or tape is known as a *database*. In large organisations, several different departments might have access to the same files but for different purposes. For example, the accounts department might need to access the sales file in order to produce bills for customers; the sales manager might wish to identify the best selling lines or the most successful sales executives.

Sometimes different files may be linked; for example, a supermarket item such as baked beans might appear in several different files, such as the *sales ledger* and the *stock file*. The database program which handles the files may need to extract data about baked beans from several different files. This is known as a *relational database*; the program which handles the files is called a *database management system*.

Similarly, in a nationwide police investigation, a relational database might allow links to be made between files of suspects in different parts of the country. A relational database allows *cross-referencing* between files.

File structure

Before files can be created by a database management system, a lot of planning is needed to design the *structure* of the file and to organise the data. Some of the points which must be considered are:

- the method of *data capture* (i.e. collection of data)
- the way the data is *input*
- the *output* needed by the user
- the need for *updating* the records
- any necessary *searching* or *sorting* of the records

A file is a set of *records*. Each record has the same structure or format as any other record. This structure consists of a number of subdivisions of the record, known as *fields*. For example:

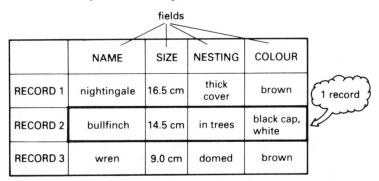

Fig. 8.2

In the above extract from a file, there are three records; each record has four fields. A record is one horizontal row of the file; a field is one vertical column.

It is normal to designate one field as the *key*; this is used for *searching* the records or *sorting* into order. For example, in a staff personnel file the *key field* might be the employee number:

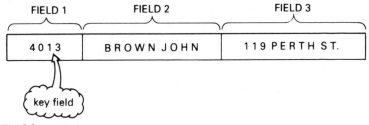

Fig. 8.3

Typical key fields in various files are:

- an employee works number
- a car registration number
- a person's National Insurance number
- a component part number
- a student's examination candidate number
- an ISBN (International Standard Book Number)

A powerful database program allows searching and sorting on any field.

In designing the file and record structure it may be necessary to design input forms on paper for *data capture*.

Before using the file-handling program, the user must decide:

- the number of fields per record
- suitable field names, e.g. SIZE, COLOUR
- the number of characters in each field
- the type of data:
  - numbers or digits – numeric data
  - letters – alphabetic data
  - letters and numbers – alphanumeric data

The commands needed to use a powerful database package are complex and are often regarded as a language in themselves. The command language for dBase III is similar to a high level programming language.

A *key-to-disk operator* types data from forms or sheets which may have been filled in by hand; these are known as *source documents*. The person who completes the data by hand at the data capture stage may have been prompted on the form by explanations for the various *codes*.

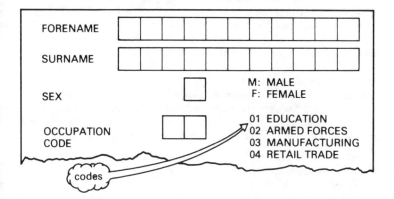

Fig. 8.4 *Data capture – source document*

The screen may be laid out in a similar way to the data capture form; this permits easy entry of data by a key-to-disk operator. To make processing of the data faster, some fields are *coded*. A fixed number of characters may be allowed for each field, for example name of bird up to 13 characters.

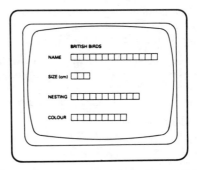

Fig. 8.5   *The screen layout for entering records in fixed-length fields*

In practice, each record might have 20 or more fields. One file might contain 30 000 records or more. There are many applications packages for handling data files; dBase II and dBase III are popular on microcomputers.

Verification
When keying-in very large quantities of data it is normal for some errors to occur in copying from the hand-written source documents. Mistakes made when copying are known as *transcription* errors. It is also quite common for people to *transpose* characters, so that 69 would become 96, for example. To eliminate copying errors, the data is re-typed by a second key-to-disk operator and any differences in the two sets of data are notified by the computer. The operator ensures that the correct version of the data is recorded on disk. Checking and correcting errors made when keying-in data from source documents onto disk or tape is known as *verification*.

Applications of databases
The database is useful in any application where sets of records are normally kept on paper. Numeric data from a database file may be 'ported' into a spreadsheet program which allows calculations, e.g. totals, averages, graphs, etc., to be carried out. Some typical uses of database files are:

● employee/student records – personal details
● libraries – records of books, authors (ISBN)
● police – criminal records
● DVLC – records of motor vehicles, drivers
● estate agent – particulars of houses

- parish records – births, deaths, marriages, etc.
- manufacturer – detailed parts lists
- sales representative – customer file
- farmer – calving, milk yields for each cow
- doctor, dentist – patients' records
- club secretary – list of members
- archaeologist – classification, archiving of historical objects
- accountant – many accounts programs are basically database management systems

The number of records must be sufficiently large to make the use of the database worthwhile; for a small number of records the manual card index system would be adequate and much cheaper.

The main tasks involved in setting up and maintaining a database are:

- *designing* the record structure
- *creating* the file – putting the record structure on disk
- *entering* and recording the data
- *searching* for particular records (*information retrieval*)
- *sorting* into order (alphabetical or numerical)
- *updating* – adding new records (*inserting* or *appending*), *amending* (altering) records, *deleting* (removing) records

When the key-to-disk operator has entered all the records, a 'dummy' record may be entered to mark the end of the data. This *dummy data* is also known as a *rogue value* or *data terminator*. The data terminator must be quite different from genuine data fields, so bizarre sets of characters are used, e.g. −999, ZZZ, etc. (otherwise the program might stop when a genuine record was mistaken for the dummy data).

At the end of data entry, the records are all written to disk or tape, and the computer may have written a *header* at the beginning of the file. At the end of the file a marker is written; the *end-of-file marker (EOF)* can be tested for later when the data is read back into memory from disk, using a *loop*, e.g. REPEAT . . . UNTIL EOF.

Fig. 8.6

The diagram suggests the storage of a file on a magnetic tape. The same concept can be used to understand a disk file, even though in practice the data may be scattered in apparently random fashion about the *sectors* and *tracks* on the disk surface.

Sequential files
These files may be stored on disk or tape; the records are stored in order, possibly using the key field such as an employee number. The records are normally accessed *serially*. This means that to read the 99th record in the file it is first necessary to read through the preceding 98.

An *indexed sequential file* (on disk) provides a separate index of the keys and their locations on disk. This file of keys can be searched more quickly than the file of complete records. The read/write head then moves to the required track or sector on the disk.

Magnetic tape permits only *serial access* and is therefore not suitable for *interactive computing* where an immediate response is required, e.g. in checking if an item is in stock in a warehouse. However, for some applications serial files on tape are quite adequate, for example:

- A payroll where a large number of records are processed routinely in the same order – *batch processing*.
- As a *backing storage* medium, for archiving large files of data from disk; for example, customer transactions in a bank. Archive data is not normally accessed for information retrieval purposes; it is simply to provide a safety net for reconstructing disk files in case of failure, or as a store for historical data which may or may not be needed in future.

Random files
In random files, the records can be accessed *directly* without reading through any previous records. The position of a record is calculated from its key field. Using *fixed-length fields* for every record it is possible to work out the exact position of any field within any record in the file.

Comparison of disk and tape files
Disk

- Disk files give faster, direct access for searching.
- Individual records and fields can be altered.

but

- Programming is complex for direct access files.

Tape

- Tape files and their associated read/write equipment are cheaper.
- Tape files may be transported easily and securely due to their compact and rugged construction.

but

- Tape files are too slow for many applications, e.g. airline booking system where files of seat reservations must always be up-to-date (*real-time system*).

KEY FACTS

Sequential files may be stored on tape or disk and require records to be accessed one after the other (serial access). Indexed sequential files on disk enable records to be found more quickly from their key fields (held in a separate file).

Random files permit direct access to individual records for reading or updating. This is done by calculating their position on a disk. Direct access is not possible on tape-based systems.

Searching

Files need to be searched in order to retrieve information urgently, for example:

- a Gas Board customer querying a bill
- a bank clerk needing to know the balance in an account
- a mechanic checking the price and availability of an exhaust system in the garage stores
- a lawyer looking for legal precedents in similar cases
- a police officer checking the ownership of an abandoned car
- a doctor seeking the antidote to a snake bite

In order to find particular records, it is necessary to enter, at a keyboard, the *search criteria*. These might simply be the key field, as in the case of a car registration number or an employee number. Since these key fields are *unique identifiers*, only one record will be found as a result of the search. However, there may be many records which match the search criteria; for example, if the name SMITH or the car make FORD were entered.

A database permits complex searches involving several fields. This reduces the number of records found (compared with searching on a single field).

Search criteria

1 | FORD | many records may be found

2 | FORD | ESCORT | fewer ESCORTS than all FORD cars

3 | FORD | ESCORT | RED | fewer records found
                                          to satisfy search
4 | FORD | ESCORT | RED | XR3 | ⟷   criteria

As more criteria are entered in the search, fewer records are found to satisfy them.

Entering the search criteria in a database may be quite complex and involve the operators AND and OR. The search criteria are normally entered at the keyboard in statements similar to the following examples:

FIND:
    MAKE EQUAL FORD <u>AND</u> MODEL EQUAL ESCORT

FIND:
    COLOUR EQUAL GREEN <u>OR</u> COLOUR EQUAL RED

Note that the use of OR will normally result in a greater number of records being found.

Numerical searches may also involve records whose fields lie within a certain range:

FIND:
    PRICE   GT   £2500   AND   PRICE   LT   £3000

Meaning:
    Print out all cars with prices between £2500 and £3000.
    (GT = greater than; LT = less than)

Searching alphabetical data may require records to be found which *begin with*, *end with* or *contain* a certain letter or group of letters.

FIND:
    SUBJECTS   CONTAIN   COM

This would display all student records which contained the letters COM in their subject field – this would include COMMERCE and COMPUTER STUDIES, for example.

Sorting
This may be done using any field, not just the key field. Sorting is necessary to enable a sequential file to be created, to enable lists to be printed in a certain order for ease of use, e.g. surnames in alphabetical order, mark lists in descending order. It is also necessary to enable a tape file to be *updated* by *merging* with a transaction file (see later).

Sorting is a very slow task when done manually and even appears to be relatively slow when done by computer. This is because sorting is done by many thousands of comparisons and swaps on the sort field; a file of a few hundred records may take several minutes to sort, even by computer. When sorting words into alphabetical order, words are compared initially on their first letters. The computer actually compares the *ASCII codes* of the letters; since A has the code 65 and B has the code 66, the mathematical operator < (less than) can also mean 'alphabetically before'.

One of the simplest sort routines is the *'bubble' sort*. The list of words is compared in pairs and the words swapped if not in alphabetical order. This process continues through a series of passes through the complete list of words until no more swaps are needed. Words 'bubble' up from the bottom of the list to find their true position. The following example describes the bubble sort using only three words; in practice several hundreds or thousands of words are sorted.

1st pass through data	polecat ⌐ zebra ⌐ aardvark	polecat zebra ⌐ aardvark ⌐
2nd pass	polecat ⌐ aardvark ⌐ zebra	aardvark polecat ⌐ zebra ⌐
3rd pass	aardvark ⌐ polecat ⌐ zebra	aardvark polecat ⌐ zebra ⌐

KEY
⌐ compared but not swapped
⌐ compared and swapped

The principle of the bubble sort

More sophisticated methods such as the *shell sort* are much faster because they make comparisons between words in opposite halves of the list (not adjacent words as in the bubble sort). This results in a much faster sorting time, but is more complex to program.

A sort routine is an example of an *algorithm* – a sequence of steps for solving a problem. A sort routine may be added to a *library* of *utility* routines needed by a programmer (but not programmed from 'scratch' (or first principles) every time).

KEY FACTS

Searching: (File Interrogation or Information Retrieval)
Finding certain records in a file, for example all
RED FORD ESCORTS.

Sorting: Arranging records in a particular order.
For example:
● people in alphabetical order of surname
● students in numerical order of examination marks

Updating a file
Computer files on disk can be altered more easily than equivalent files on paper. Files of data stored on magnetic tape cannot be altered directly; a new file on a different tape is created by merging the changes with the old tape file. The updating of tape files is discussed in detail later.

An example of a file which needs periodic updating would be a name and address file for a swimming club. The following changes would be needed to keep the file up-to-date:
1   New members would join the club, so records would be added to the file; *appending* means placing new records at the end of the file; *inserting* means placing records between existing records in the file.

2 From time to time members would leave the club, so their records would be *deleted* (removed from the file).

3 The details of some members would change, so their records would be amended (*altered* or *modified*). Typical amendments would be a change of address, telephone number, marital status, name, etc.

Using a disk system, the original file can be updated, since the precise records and fields can be located on the disk and overwritten with the new data (or deletions). A tape file cannot be accessed accurately in this way, so updating a file using the same tape is not practicable. A database which can be updated immediately is said to be *on-line*; the terminal providing access to the database is connected directly to the computer.

Real-time

Databases which are always up-to-date are said to operate in *real-time*. These are necessary in applications where several users may have access to the same database.

Examples of real-time databases are:

- airline booking system
- theatre booking system
- some stock control systems

These systems have a central computer accessed by a large number of *terminals*. It is essential that staff using many different terminals don't all try to sell the same items, such as theatre seats or aircraft seats; similarly a terminal in a large store or warehouse should always show the correct number of items in stock. Therefore updating of the computer files must be immediate or in real-time.

KEY FACTS

Updating a file

Inserting, appending:	adding new records
Deleting:	removing unwanted records
Amending:	altering details of existing records
On-line devices:	connected to the central computer directly; for example, a terminal for updating a database
Real-time database:	a database which is updated immediately – there is negligible time delay between entering the amendments and the files being modified

---

Merging files

The tape file cannot be updated by finding a particular record and then changing it. Unlike a point on a disk which can be identified by its track and sector number, there is no way of accurately locating a point on a tape. A completely new file must be created on a separate tape. In some applications this is an advantage since the old data file remains intact as a backup copy (in case the new file is lost or damaged).

Where a very large number of changes occur in a day or a week (as in a shop), it is normal to create a separate file of all the changes. The file containing the changes is known as the *transaction file*; the main file containing the entire set of records is known as the *master file*.

Applications where a system of master and transaction files may be used are:

- the stock control system in a large company, supermarket
- the Driver and Vehicle Licensing Centre (DVLC)
- a payroll system (wages)
- a large library

In a supermarket the day's sales might be input onto tape using *Kimball tags*; new stock will also be delivered to the warehouse. Items sold, together with new stock, form the data for the transaction file stored on tape. The transaction data must be sorted into the same order as the main or master file. The two files are then *merged* to create a new file.

Provided the two files are in the same order, merging is fairly straightforward. Records from the transaction file and master file are read into memory one at a time and their keys compared. The records are then written to the new master file in the correct order.

The three generations of files (grandfather–father–son system)

Merging of files on tape produces a secure system of data storage; a new master file and the old master file and transaction file all exist on separate tapes. In practice, it is normal to keep the three latest versions of the master file, together with the transaction files. The method of keeping the three latest copies of files for security purposes is known as the *grandfather–father–son* system – the grandfather representing the oldest file, etc. If the latest file is lost or damaged it can be reconstructed from the earlier file and the transaction file.

Batch processing

A system which takes large quantities of similar data and works through systematically is known as a batch processing system. A large collection of Kimball tags could be processed overnight by a batch processing system. Unlike the real-time system, the batch processing system is not up-to-date until the outstanding batches of data have all been processed.

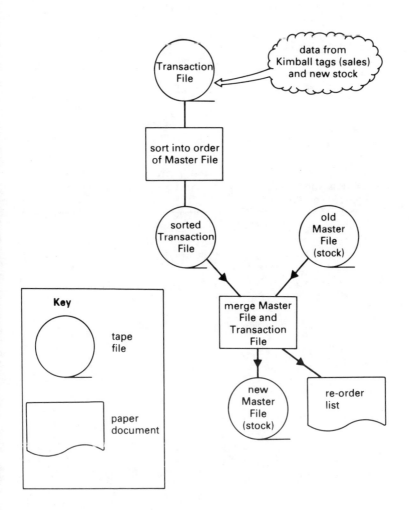

Fig. 8.7   *Merging transaction files and master files – a systems flowchart*

Examples of batch processing:

- credit card vouchers collected from shops, garages all over the country (processed overnight at a bank)
- calculating and printing employees' wage slips
- producing regular bills (say quarterly), e.g. gas, electricity, rates
- marking examination scripts by computer
- processing records at the DVLC
- the weekly processing of a collection of sales invoices.

KEY FACTS
Batch Processing
The processing of a large number or batch of similar items after collection from a variety of sources. There is a delay between the collection of the data and the updating of the files, so batch processing is used for non-urgent data.

Database systems normally consist of a *suite* of programs. Apart from the programs to *create* and *maintain* the files, there are programs which *check* that the data being input is sensible.

Validation checks are intended to ensure that the data is suitable for the purpose for which it is being used; in particular that data is:

* of the correct *type* (alphabetic, numeric, etc.)
* within an acceptable numerical *range*

Examples of validation *type* checks:

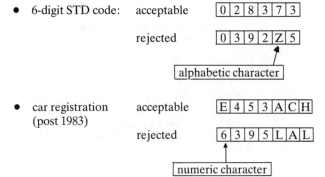

Examples of validation *range* checks:

* school students/pupils ages: $5 \leqslant age \leqslant 19$
* examination percentages: $0 \leqslant marks \leqslant 100$
* date written in figures: acceptable 30/11/53
  (dd/mm/yy) rejected 49/08/62

  too many days in the month

In the case of range checks, an acceptable range may be based on a previous reading. For example, a gas bill may be compared with the same period in the previous year; any great difference would suggest an error in the data.

Validation checks do not guarantee that all input data is correct; some errors would not be found by validation. For example, an employee's age would normally lie within the range 16 to 65 years. Suppose a key-to-disk operator was meant to enter 34 but instead entered 43 – a *transposition* error. The age entered is *incorrect* but not *invalid* – it is still within the acceptable range. The validation check would not reject this data; however, a *verification* check should detect this type of error.

> **Validation checks** must be combined with **verification checks** to reduce the number of errors in data input and ensure the integrity (accuracy and completeness) of the data.

A number of further validation checks may be applied to numeric data to improve the accuracy. Two of these methods include *totalling* the numbers both *before* and *after* the numbers are input to the computer – any difference in the two totals suggests (though does not prove) an error in the entry of the data.

The hash total
A meaningless total is calculated by adding a series of numbers – which may not have any mathematical meaning; for example:

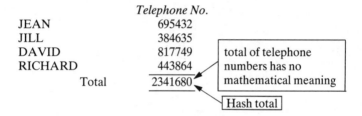

	Telephone No.
JEAN	695432
JILL	384635
DAVID	817749
RICHARD	443864
Total	2341680

total of telephone numbers has no mathematical meaning

Hash total

The numbers *and their total* are entered into the computer. The program *recalculates the total* and compares this with the total entered with the data. If the two totals are the same, this indicates that the data has been entered correctly (see Fig. 8.8).

But:
The hash total could be the same after data entry if two or more errors were made which *cancelled* each other out.

Examples of hash totals:

- employee numbers
- bank account numbers
- dates of birth
- telephone numbers
- examination candidate numbers

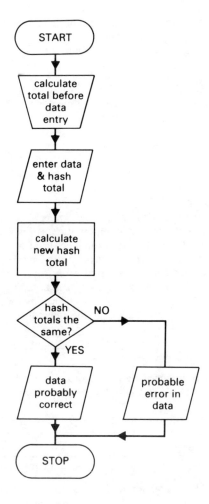

Fig. 8.8

Control total

This is similar to a hash total, except that the control total is a genuine total of 'mathematical' numbers.

For example, in a wages program:

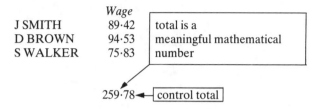

	Wage	
J SMITH	89·42	total is a
D BROWN	94·53	meaningful mathematical
S WALKER	75·83	number

259·78 ◄── control total

Check digits

This is a method of checking that numbers have been input correctly; it is applied to *identification numbers* such as bank account and credit card numbers and also the ISBN numbers used on books. The *check digit* is calculated from digits in a newly allocated number; this is added to the end of the number and recalculated every time the number is input to the computer. One method is the *weighted modulo 11* test. Suppose the next available account number for a bank customer was 93452. The check digit must be calculated and added to the end to form a 6-digit account number.

9 3 4 5 2 ☐ ◄── check digit goes here

Calculating the check digit – weighted modulo 11 method

Each digit of 93452 is multiplied by a *weighting* starting with 2 on the right.

incomplete account number	9 3 4 5 2
weightings	6 5 4 3 2
products	$54 + 15 + 16 + 15 + 4 = 104$

$104 \div 11$ gives remainder 5

check digit $= 11 - 5 = 6$

The complete account number becomes 93452 6 ◄────── check digit

Whenever this account number is input to the computer, the weighted modulo 11 test is repeated and the total should be divisible by 11.

final account number	9 3 4 5 2 6
weightings	6 5 4 3 2 1
products	$54 + 15 + 16 + 15 + 4 + 6 = 110$

$110 \div 11$ gives remainder 0, therefore number is correct since weighted total is divisible by 11.

The check digit is widely used and catches most faulty numbers at the input stage. It may be possible in a few cases to make an error which results in an incorrect number not detected by the check digit method. By *coincidence* the incorrect number may also satisfy the weighted modulo 11 test. However, in large computer systems a complete range of validation and verification checks ensures that most, if not all, incorrect data is detected at the input stage.

Files must be kept safe because:

- the data may be *essential* for the running of an organisation or business, e.g. customer files, addresses, sales ledger, payroll files, technical design details (industrial espionage)
- the data may be *private* and *confidential* – health records, career details, personal or family history

The loss of computer files may result in a company being forced out of business; at the very least it will require large quantities of data to be re-keyed, involving considerable time and expense.

Accidental loss of data

Computer users should keep at least three copies of all important files; if only two are kept, all data may be lost if the disks are copied in the wrong sequence (or a faulty disk is copied from). Backing-up in this way includes the grandfather–father–son method in which the three latest versions (or three generations) of tape files are kept. During the periodic saving or writing of the files on tape, three different tapes are used in *rotation*; a new file is written on what was previously the grandfather – this becomes the son. The previous father becomes the grandfather; the previous son becomes the father.

Disk files may be protected from deletion by a software operation known as *locking*. A locked file may only be deleted by a person with sufficient authority – the *system manager*.

A disk containing important data may be protected from accidental deletion by fitting a *write-protect tab*, which must be removed before the contents of the disk can be altered. In a similar way, tapes are protected by the need to fit a *write-permit ring* before files can be *deleted* or *overwritten*. The latest 3·5in disks use a small write-protect 'switch' built into the disk.

It is normal for important files to be copied and the original stored in a safe place in a different building – in case of fire, floods, etc.

Errors due to computer faults are relatively uncommon. Faults in the program or data are more common – *GIGO (Garbage In, Garbage Out)*. However, a program can be damaged by temporary *surges* in the electrical power supply; these are known as '*spikes*' and the program may be protected by the fitting of special *anti-surge devices*. Large installations may have *standby generators* in case of power cuts or even *duplicate computer systems* in another town. *Computer bureaux* (firms which undertake computing work for other companies) may be used by firms whose own computer system has failed.

Computer crime

Crime involving computers is an increasing problem. It is very difficult to detect since there are no obvious signs of burglary or forced entry. Also, the complexity of computer systems may prevent anyone other than specialist programmers from understanding the true situation. Many of the police will not have the specialist training to investigate a computer crime thoroughly; barristers and judges have difficulty in interpreting the law because of *computer jargon*. There are few, if any, legal precedents for some types of computer crime.

The recent trial of computer *'hackers'* – who read private electronic mailbox files by obtaining and entering the real owners' *passwords* – was prosecuted as a case of *forgery*. The legal debate revolved around the nature of the crime, if indeed one had been committed.

Other crimes are clear cases of *theft* or *criminal damage*, e.g. copying a disk or wiping it clean. One of the most common crimes is to copy disks which have been carelessly left on an office desk. *Software piracy* is a crime which involves a few pounds for a home computer game or several hundred pounds for a 'pirate' copy of a wordprocessor program. Piracy is believed to cost the computer software industry many millions of pounds in lost sales; it is claimed that this software theft may threaten the jobs of many computing staff – if not the survival of the *software houses* themselves.

In practice, most major computer crimes involve financial institutions (banks, etc.) and are committed from the *inside*, i.e. by employees. In the *'salami'* method, a person enriches their own account by transferring to it a very large number of small amounts from many other accounts. There are no obvious victims, since no one person loses a significant amount of money.

Other computer crimes may include damage to software by *disgruntled employees* – by planting *'bugs'* in a program. A further crime is the spreading of a *'virus'*, or *logic bomb*; this is a method of vandalising software by planting a few lines of programming which corrupt disks after a certain length of time. The virus can be spread by the copying of disks. The biggest threat is that viruses could be used to damage banking systems or the computer programs used to control nuclear missiles.

Computer crime may be minimised by limiting the access to the computer room to certain trusted individuals. Security guards are employed on large installations. Keys may be necessary to unlock the computer itself.

Within the computer, *passwords* may be necessary to access certain files. In addition, various *levels of access* may restrict the reading of files to certain users; files may be *'locked'* so that they cannot be accidentally deleted or unlocked by an unauthorised user. Passwords should be *changed* frequently and should not be written down; the password should not be simple, e.g. a person's birthdate could easily be 'hacked'.

It should be noted that deleting of files may not prevent the data being read later by an unscrupulous user. Deleting does not actually remove a file from a disk immediately – only the file *name* is removed from the *catalogue*. So the data may be resurrected at a later date if it has not been overwritten.

Encryption is a method of *encoding* data into a meaningless jumble. The data can only be '*unscrambled*' by the use of the correct program for *decoding*.

Electronic eavesdropping consists of the reading of computer screens from a distance of several hundred metres away. Special equipment is available which intercepts the *microwaves* emitted by the computer screen; one method of preventing this is to coat the office windows with a special metallic film.

Summary

Precautions against accidental loss or damage to data

- Make back-up copies of important files.
- Keep transaction data (the changes needed for updating).
- Rotate the files in the grandfather–father–son system (three generations of files).
- Store copies in a separate building (as a precaution against fire, flood, etc.).
- Protect against power failures or fluctuations (standby generators, anti-surge devices, duplicate computer systems, arrangement with other organisations, computer bureaux).
- Protect disk files from accidental damage by 'write-protect' tabs or switches; use 'write-permit' rings on magnetic tapes.
- Use software protection to 'lock' files, or give read-only access.

Precautions against criminal theft or damage to data

- Use passwords to limit access to the system.
- Change passwords regularly; use passwords which are not obvious.
- Restrict access to certain files to particular users.
- Keep important disks, tapes, locked away when not in use.
- Maintain good staff relations (to prevent damage by disgruntled employees).
- Choose staff carefully for positions of trust.
- Encode important files (encryption) – special decoding programs needed to unscramble the data.
- Protect computer and buildings from electronic eavesdropping of microwaves.
- Build protection routines into programs to prevent illegal copying (software piracy). Use special programs to prevent the spread of 'viruses' or 'logic bombs'.
- Restrict physical access to the computer – locks on the room, identity passes for the building, keys to access the terminal.

1   Choose two words from the given list to complete the sentence.

disks   fields   records   tapes

A file is a set of . . . each of which has . . .

(MEG Specimen Paper 1, Section G, Qu. 5)

2   A shop keeps details of all the items it sells, as shown below.

Description	Quantity	Unit cost	Supplier	
Biro pen	37	5	A2	
HB pencil	100	2	B3	
HH pencil	75	3	B3	Box A
Ruler 30 cm	120	10	D1	
Rubber	78	6	D1	Box B

Choose words from the list to complete the sentences.

file   record   field   character

(*a*) Box A contains a . . .
(*b*) Box B contains a . . .

(LEAG Specimen Paper 1, Qu. 2)

3   A garage has a database which keeps details of items in stock. Describe *three* fields you would expect to find in each record.

(MEG Specimen Paper 1, Section E, Qu. 16)

4   Explain the terms *serial access* and *direct access*.

5   A file holds records of pupils. Two details which are kept are the name and year of birth of each pupil. Describe *two* checks which could be used to validate a record.

(MEG Specimen Paper 1, Section F, Qu. 11)

6   Which of these applications could most conveniently use a serial access file?
A producing payslips **B** running students' programs from terminals **C** a program library **D** information retrieval

(SEG Specimen Paper 1, Qu. 7)

7   When stock arrives at a warehouse, items which have not previously been held in stock are given new code numbers and new records and are then added to the stock file. The stock file is held in order of code number. Explain the use of SORT and MERGE routines to do this.

(MEG Specimen Paper 3, Section B, Qu. 2)

8 An additional digit calculated from an account number and placed at the end of it could be used as a

A check digit **B** parity digit **C** parity bit **D** sign bit **E** rogue value

(NISEC Specimen Paper 3, Section A, Qu. 3)

9 The security of the information in a computer file is important. Describe *one* way of preventing the wrong person gaining access to a file.

(LEAG Specimen Paper 3, Qu. 5)

10 (*a*) Explain what is meant by the term 'file' as used in data processing.

(*b*) The information on a company's master file is very valuable and must not be damaged or lost. State *one* precaution that should be taken to guard against this.

(WJEC Specimen Paper 1, Qu. 9)

11 A school keeps a file containing pupils' names. Give an example where:

(*a*) a name would need to be inserted in the file;

(*b*) a name would need to be amended;

(*c*) a name would need to be deleted from the file.

(*d*) The school keeps the information on a computer disk. How can they avoid losing all the information if the disk is accidentally damaged?

(LEAG Specimen Paper 1, Qu. 18)

12 A school keeps computer records of pupils' personal details. Give *two* safeguards which may be used to stop possible misuse of this data.

13 In which of these is a transaction file most likely to be used?

A updating **B** merging **C** sorting **D** copying

(SEG Specimen Paper 1, Qu. 22)

14 (*a*) *Verification* and *validation* both refer to checking of data. Explain the difference between them.

(*b*) Which one would be more likely to be carried out off-line? Say why you think this is so.

(*c*) Items in a catalogue each have a 3-digit code number, e.g. 327. A fourth digit is to be added as a check digit. It will be worked out according to a set of rules.

Give an example of a set of rules which could be used.

If a check digit shows an error, why does the computer not correct it and then carry on?

(SEB Ordinary Grade 1986 Section 1, Qu. 9)

15 When gas meters are read the meter reader sends the readings to the Gas Board's computer centre.

The data preparation staff then key in the meter readings and customer account numbers into a computer via terminals.

This information is then verified and stored on disc as the READINGS FILE.

(*a*) Describe one method of data verification.

(*b*) The OLD MASTER CUSTOMER FILE is held on tape and stored in customer account number order.

The READINGS FILE is sorted into customer account number order before being used to update the OLD MASTER CUSTOMER FILE.

A NEW MASTER CUSTOMER FILE and bills are produced.

The same process is also shown in the diagram below.

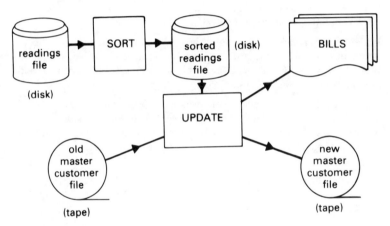

Fig. 8.9

Explain why the READINGS FILE is sorted into customer account number order before being processed against the OLD MASTER CUSTOMER FILE.

(*c*) Explain why the OLD MASTER CUSTOMER FILE and the READINGS FILE are kept after the NEW MASTER CUSTOMER FILE has been created.

(SEB Standard Grade 1988 Credit Level, Qu. 5)

Communication is the exchange of *information* between people. Computers are used as huge stores of information (databases) and these can be linked electronically to allow many people to have access to the information; humans may *interact* with the database so that they become both *receivers* and *providers* of information. Computers may be linked to allow the *transmission* and *receiving* of messages as an alternative to the telephone and the letter post, giving a faster and more versatile service. The linking of computers in this way is often referred to as *communications* and the complete system of linked computers is referred to as a *network*. There are two basic types of network, depending on the distances over which the terminals or workstations are spread. These are the *Wide Area Network (WAN)* and the *Local Area Network (LAN)*.

Wide Area Network   A system of several hundred (or thousand) computers or *terminals* connected to a central computer via the telecommunications network. Information may be transmitted and received both nationally and globally (via satellite).

Local Area Network   A system of perhaps 10–250 computers or terminals linked together by special cabling on the same site. Such a network would typically be spread over a distance of up to half a mile around a college or school campus, or the offices of a large organisation (local authority, hospital, bank, newspaper, etc.).

A *gateway* allows networks to be linked to each other; for example, a local area network might be linked to the telephone wide area network and then to another local network.

The data which is transmitted may take the form of text (as in the case of normal letters and correspondence); this is known as *electronic mail*. Or the user may interrogate a database (*information retrieval*); this is analogous to withdrawing a book from the library. However, in the database the information is constantly *updated* – unlike a textbook, which may take over a year to produce. The data transmitted may also be in the form of *computer software* (programs), which may be 'downloaded' and *saved* on disk. This is much easier than retyping a program from a listing on paper (but may involve copyright problems).

The existing telephone network is the basis of most electronic communications networks. This includes millions of miles of copper cabling installed around the world and under the sea. In addition, data may be transmitted as *microwaves* via *satellite* to all parts of the world.

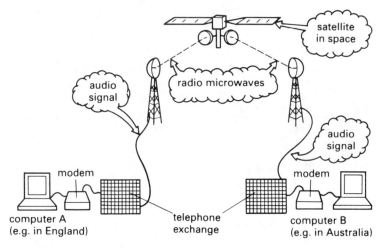

Fig. 9.1 *An international communications network*

The components of a wide area network

The terminals or *workstations* may be microcomputers; in this case they are '*intelligent*' *terminals* since they have some independent processing power. Some terminals are simply input and output devices (keyboard + screen) and are known as '*dumb*' *terminals*. The *teletypewriter* is a keyboard with a small integral printer. The terminals are connected via the network to a '*host*' mainframe computer. This may allow connection to other computer networks via gateways; the gateways may allow connection to the databases of the *information providers* such as the Meteorological Office or the Stock Exchange.

The data is transmitted around the network in small groups or *packets*. These are directed through a series of exchanges where they are switched to their destination. This is known as the *Packet Switched Stream (PSS)*. The PSS enables data to be transmitted throughout Great Britain at the same rate of charges as local telephone calls.

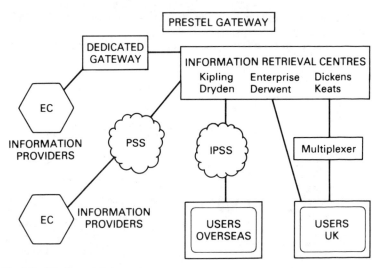

Fig. 9.2 *The Prestel Gateway*

Modems and acoustic couplers

A wide area network can be accessed by a small microcomputer. Special software is needed to handle the signals; this enables connections to be made between computers according to a special *protocol* or set of rules. The computer transmits signals in *binary* form (0s and 1s) and these must be converted to *audio* signals for transmission along the telephone network. The device used to convert binary signals to audio is either a *modem* (modulator/demodulator) or an *acoustic coupler*.

The copper cable used for the telephone network may eventually be replaced by *fibre optic cables*; these permit greater speed of data transfer by using lasers to transmit data in the form of pulses of light. Fibre optics make possible the transmission of data in digital form (0s and 1s).

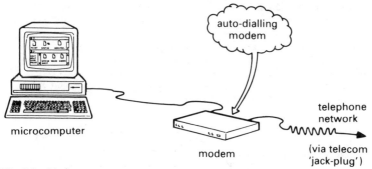

Fig. 9.3 *Modem*

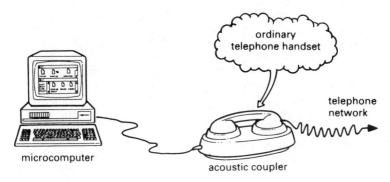

Fig. 9.4 *Acoustic coupler*

Joining a network

It is necessary to pay an annual *subscription* to join one of the major networks such as:

- Telecom Gold for business users
- Prestel for business and education (includes Micronet for home computer owners)
- TTNS (The Times Network System) for schools and colleges
- Teletel – the French national system.

Information providers
The subscriber to a network pays a fee to the organisers of the network. This fee covers the cost of providing the service and the central computer which holds the databases – the 'host' computer

In addition, fees may be payable to the information providers – sometimes chargeable per *page* of information (one page being a 'screenful' of information). Typical information provided includes:

● the Stock Exchange – share prices
● the Meteorological Office – weather forecasts
● agriculture – news on crops, prices, pests (Prestel Farmlink)
● educational resources for teachers, TTNS, NERIS Database
● careers information for students

Systems such as Prestel are known as *videotex* services. Prestel offers over 300 000 pages of information to users.

The French Teletel system has a very large number of users, probably because the Minitel terminals needed to access the system were provided free – as an alternative to telephone directories. This saves the time needed in updating, printing and distributing new directories in book form. Teletel allows any person's telephone number to be found by a *keyword search*; the user simply types the name and town of the person to be contacted and the system immediately responds with their telephone number. In addition, a wide range of videotex services is available from information providers to Teletel:

● home shopping
● home banking and insurance
● gamcs and 'chat' facilities
● computer dating

Using databases
There are two basic methods of interrogating these large databases:

● through a series of menus
● by entering the words you wish to find – the keyword search

Searching using menus
When using a series of menus the user progressively approaches the chosen subject. For example, to find out about Information Technology in Secondary Schools it might be necessary to take the following route through the menus:

1   Select Education
2   Select Secondary
3   Select Curriculum
4   Select Information Technology

The keyword search
In the keyword search, the user would simply enter Information Technology and the computer would respond with all references to the subject.

Videotex
A feature of the videotex service is that it is possible for the user to interact with the database; a student might interrogate the UCCA database to find out about university places available, then respond by making an application electronically via the keyboard. Other *interactive* services allow goods to be ordered electronically; or travel agents may examine holiday vacancies and then make a booking.

Teletext
Certain databases may be accessed by the owner of a television with a special *teletext adapter*; teletext is *not interactive*, the user is only able to *receive information*. Pages of information are selected by using a special keypad. The pages cover topics such as news, sport, weather forecasts and television programmes. The main teletext services are *Ceefax (BBC)* and *Oracle (ITV)*.

Electronic mail
Subscribers to a network system such as Prestel, TTNS or Telecom Gold have access to an *electronic mail system*; this enables the *sending* and *receiving* of *documents*. Electronic mail has a number of advantages over the conventional postal and telephone services.

- Electronic mail is very *fast* (delivered almost instantly).
- There is no problem with people whose phone is engaged or who may be out of the office; the mail goes straight into their *electronic mailbox*. This is in the central host computer, perhaps in London or New York.
- Correspondence may be *recorded on disk* or printed on paper at the receiving end.
- One document can easily be sent to a very large number of recipients.
- The sender may be informed as soon as important messages have been read – an *acknowledgement* is automatically sent (if requested).
- An immediate *reply* may be requested.
- *Computer software (programs)* may be transmitted and *downloaded* directly to disk.

User groups
On subscribing to a network, the user receives an *identity number* and a *password*. The user is advised to change the password regularly. The User Identity Number gives access to a *mailbox* in the host computer. Anyone wishing to send a message to another user must know their identity in order to place a document in their mailbox.

It should be noted that electronic mail does not usually take the form of direct contact between two computer users. Mail is placed in the recipient's mailbox in the host computer. It remains there until the recipient reads the mail and eventually deletes it.

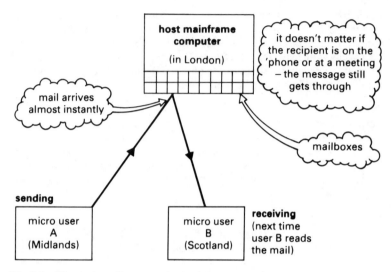

Fig. 9.5   *Electronic mail: communication between typical users*

Electronic mail has many important applications. Apart from well-established systems in the field of banking (discussed later), it provides an important method of communication for users in business and education.

KEY FACTS

Teletext services (Ceefax, Oracle) only allow data to be *received*; transmission is in *one direction*.

Videotex services (Prestel, TTNS) are *interactive*; data may be received and *transmitted* by the user.

Journalism
A journalist working on remote assignments can use a *portable* computer to produce copy (or text) using a *wordprocessing* program, and *save* it as a *file*. The computer may then be connected to a telephone line and the file of text transmitted to the newspaper office by electronic mail. Long documents should be produced 'off-line' using a wordprocessor. This is because the wordprocessor has powerful *editing* (or correcting) facilities that are not available when typing directly 'on-line' via the modem. Typing directly on-line through the modem can waste time and money and produce text which is full of mistakes.

Sales
A *sales representative* might use a portable computer linked to the telephone network by a modem; for example to send a nightly statement of new *orders*, while working a long way from the office. This would be easier than telephoning the data and faster than sending the orders by post. Similarly, *pharmacists* make bulk orders for drugs by electronic mail; these can be printed out at the wholesalers and the printout used to make up the required batches of drugs from the warehouse shelves.

Newspaper/magazine distribution
Using similar principles to electronic mail, it is now possible to transmit the text of newspapers electronically from the editorial offices to regional *printing units*. This removes the need to physically transport the printed newspapers by rail or lorry from London to the regions. A further development of newspaper production is the possibility of transmitting the newspaper text directly into the *home*, where it would be read on the television screen or computer monitor. Any pages of special interest could be printed out on paper.

Working from home
Some people now *work at home* and transmit their work to the office via electronic mail. Suitable jobs for this pattern of working are computer programmers, accountants, authors, scientists and typists.

Education
A school or college can send out a message and direct it automatically to all other similar institutions in the same area. This would be useful for arranging sports fixtures, for example, or requesting the loan of specialist books or equipment.

Advantages of electronic mail
(compared with conventional methods, e.g. letter post, telephone)

- Text is delivered almost instantly over long distances (including internationally).
- Unlike the telephone, there is no need to make personal contact with someone who may be otherwise engaged.
- Electronic mail is quite cheap (usually at local telephone rates) and saves the time and cost of envelopes, stamps, etc.
- Large quantities of text may be transmitted and permanently saved electronically at the receiving end.
- The text can be read into a wordprocessor, etc., and edited or modified.
- Computer software (programs) may be transmitted and 'downloaded' straight onto disk.
- Copies may easily be sent to a very large circulation list, with acknowledgement of receipt.

There are no real disadvantages of electronic mail but the following may be thought of as 'costs' of the system:

- A computer system and telephone line must be provided and fees paid to maintain the system and join a user group.
- A person must be trained to use the system and spend a regular part of the working day in sending mail and distributing incoming mail to the various recipients.
- The use of electronic mail replaces direct personal contact between people; people working from home via electronic mail may feel isolated and miss contact with colleagues.
- The system must be carefully managed to prevent misuse; examples of misuse include the transmission of obscene or unwelcome material.

The fax (facsimile) machine

The fax machine enables *any* sort of document to be transmitted, whether it is typed, handwritten or *graphics* (pictures). The sender calls up the fax machine at the receiving end; the document is scanned and converted to electrical signals. These are transmitted down the telephone line. At the receiving end the electrical signals are converted back to a picture and printed out.

Fig. 9.6 *The fax machine*

Unlike electronic mail, fax machines cannot store the images of documents on disk for subsequent computer processing. It is really like transmitting photocopies over long distances. However, fax machines are fast and can handle pictures, which electronic mail cannot.

Fax may be used for rapidly transmitting copies of important documents; banks use this method to send urgent copies of specimen signatures between branches. Newspapers and magazines use fax machines to transmit photographs.

Telex

Telex is a relatively old system and allows text to be transmitted worldwide by a network of telegraph cables. Telex machines are similar to teletypewriters, enabling messages to be sent and received (and printed automatically) on a *one-to-one* basis. The sender must first call up the machine which is to receive the message or text. Tele*tex* (not Tele*text*) is a modern telex system offering more facilities.

Apart from the general facilities of wide area networks, namely *electronic mail* and *videotex systems*, a number of more specialised applications have been developed.

Banking
The banks have used networks and terminals for some years to provide information on a global scale.

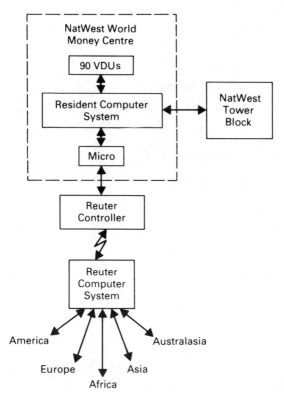

Fig. 9.7 *An international banking network*

The computerised dealing system at the London Foreign Exchange gives dealers immediate VDU displays of *exchange rates* for currencies throughout the world.

Two major banking networks are known as *SWIFT* and *CHAPS*. SWIFT is the Society for Worldwide Inter-Bank Financial Telecommunications. This allows payments representing very large sums of money to be transferred between 1000 banks all over the world. For security, the data is *scrambled* (made incomprehensible) by *coding* or *encryption*. CHAPS is the Clearing House Automated Payment System, and enables payments of large sums of money to be 'cleared' or approved on the same day within the United Kingdom.

Automated Teller Machines (ATMs)

ATMs (also known as *cash dispensers*) allow customers to carry out certain banking transactions outside of normal banking hours; they also relieve the pressure on the bank's cashiers during normal banking hours. This enables bank staff to carry out other duties, e.g. improving customer relations or marketing activities. The customer uses a 'hole in the wall' terminal connected to the bank's main computer by the telephone network.

personal identification number (PIN) keyed in for security

Fig. 9.8   *Automated Teller Machine (ATM) or cash dispenser*

The customer inserts a *magnetic stripe card* containing their account number, etc.; at the same time the customer must enter a *Personal Identification Number (PIN)* by keying it in separately. The PIN is a safeguard against theft and should therefore be kept secret.

Amongst the services offered by Automated Teller Machines are:

- withdrawing cash
- checking the balance in an account
- ordering a bank statement

The main computers at the bank's computer centre are automatically updated with the transactions from the ATMs. Apart from the convenience to customers, the system is fast and efficient, reducing the amount of paperwork handled by the bank's staff. A disadvantage might be the lack of personal contact between cashiers and customers, and the possibility of 'mugging' in a High Street situation.

Home banking

The Home and Office Banking Service (HOBS) is operated jointly by the Bank of Scotland and Prestel via the telephone network. This enables users to carry out certain banking transactions using either a microcomputer and a modem, or a special Prestel/HOBS keyboard. The advantages of the system include the fact that the user does not have to leave home (or the office) and the service is also available outside normal banking hours, seven days a week.

The service enables the user to:

- transfer money from one account to another
- order statements and new cheque books
- check balances and recent transactions

| Personal | or | Business |

Fig. 9.9 *The Bank of Scotland Home and Office Banking Service*

By transferring money between current and investment accounts it is possible for the user to maximise the interest on their savings – while ensuring that there is always enough money in the current account to meet any bills.

This service is potentially very useful for disabled or housebound people or those too busy to visit the bank in person.

The Prestel Teleshopping scheme allows the home user to order goods without leaving home, the goods being delivered within a day. It is also possible to use Prestel to buy or sell shares on the Stock Exchange.

Electronic Funds Transfer at Point of Sale (EFTPOS)

Work is in hand to extend the use of magnetic stripe cards to enable electronic payment for goods at point of sale terminals in shops. Delay in introducing the system has been caused partly by the expense of developing new terminals (or adapting existing ones). One possible medium is the Smart Card, a plastic card about the size of the magnetic stripe card which contains an internal microchip and memory.

Business transactions by large companies and banks have been conducted electronically for years – accounts are debited and credited without any cash physically changing hands. EFTPOS involves the electronic debiting of the customer's account (and crediting of the retailer's account) – the only paper produced being the receipt.

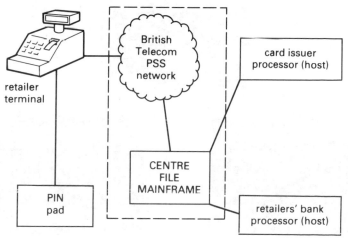

Fig. 9.10 *The EFTPOS system under development by the National Westminster Bank*

The sequence of operations is as follows:

- The cashier lists the items and the total price.
- The customer wipes the plastic card through a special reader.
- The information is transmitted via the telephone network to the card issuer (i.e. the customer's bank). The issuer agrees (or not) to the amount.
- The customer types the PIN at the terminal and this is verified by the issuer. The terminal issues a receipt.
- The system subsequently debits the customer's account and credits the account of the retailer.
- The processing cycle will still be three days – the same as for a traditional paper cheque.

Advantages of EFTPOS

The EFTPOS system is still at the experimental stage, with pilot trials to assess customers' response and to highlight any problems. However, the system clearly has many advantages:

To the customer

- It is fast and convenient.
- It is secure – card thieves also need to know the separate PIN number and there is a 'hot card' file for stolen cards.
- High value goods can be taken away immediately by the customer.
- There is no need to carry cash or cheques

To the retailer

- Faster throughput at the checkout terminals.
- Guaranteed payment at the time of purchase.
- Less paperwork, cash totalling, etc.
- Less cash to hold, lower risk of robbery, fraud.
- Linking of terminals to the head office computer gives improved stock control and management information on sales.

Retailers are compelled by law to offer customers a variety of methods of payment. However, it seems certain that the speed and convenience of EFTPOS will increase its usage, and reduce the amount of cash and cheques in circulation.

Many processes, such as those used in the chemical industry, require a continuous surveillance of important measurements or *parameters*. If, for example, a pressure or temperature exceeds the safe working *limit*, then *corrective action* must be taken – either to restore the process to satisfactory operation or to shut the process down in a safe and controlled manner.

Such a process is the transportation of crude oil from the sea port at Rotterdam by pipeline to various parts of West Germany. The pipeline is continuously *monitored* by a network of microprocessors situated at several stations across the Netherlands and West Germany. The microprocessors measure parameters or limits such as pipeline pressure, to detect faults or cracks in the pipe. The operators at the monitoring station check VDU displays of the system, including alarm signals which require corrective action to be taken.

Consumption of electricity is also recorded in the different regions and the running time of pump motors is *logged* for maintenance purposes. The data captured at the outstations is transmitted via the network to a minicomputer where it is saved (*archived*) on magnetic tape for future analysis. The minicomputer is duplicated for security purposes in what is

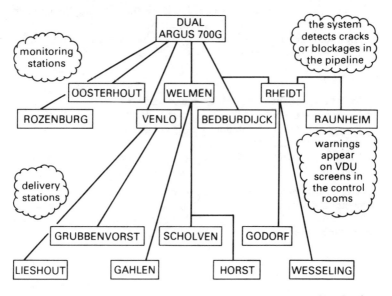

Fig. 9.11 *Monitoring a pipeline using a network (the Rotterdam–Rhine Pipeline Project)*

known as the *Master and Standby Computer* configuration. Should the Master fail for any reason, the Standby Computer automatically takes control of the network.

The system is based around the Ferranti Argus minicomputer, supporting a network of microprocessors at the outstations.

Data logging using networks

Data logging is the collection of scientific or statistical data using *automatic sensors* for input to a computer.

In order to plan for the traffic requirements in the years ahead, the government monitors the amount of traffic at various census points across the country. A computer-based system provides a fast and accurate method of capturing and classifying the data. Sensors on the road detect the presence of vehicles, the width of their axles, and the speed at which they are travelling. This data is *classified* by a microprocessor before being transmitted to the data collection centre via a modem and the telephone network. Here a minicomputer is used to convert the data into meaningful information from which plans can be made for the national road network of the future.

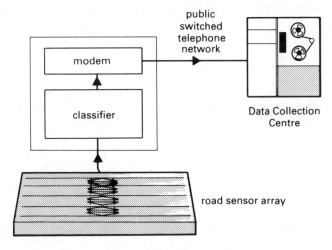

Fig. 9.12 *Data logging using a network (traffic census)*

The *local area network* is a system of terminals linked by wiring around a central computer on a single site. The terminals may be simple VDUs + keyboards or they may be microcomputers. The site is normally a suite of business offices, a hospital, university, college or school campus. In a school it may be feasible to run a network of only 10 microcomputers, while a large college might have as many as 250 machines. An industrial organisation or university might have a network consisting of hundreds of terminals attached to a central mainframe or minicomputer. This is known as a *multi-access* system.

Various advantages are gained by using a network:

- Many users can gain access to expensive *peripheral devices* such as printers and disk drives. The alternative is to equip each machine with its own disk drive and printer. These are known as *standalone* systems and are obviously much more expensive.
- Many people can use a *single copy* of an expensive piece of *software*. (In this case, a special version of the software should be purchased, with a *network licence*.) In a school computer room, it might be too expensive to buy, say, 15 copies of a £50 software package and *illegal* to make *multiple copies* of one original.
- Many users can access the same set of *data*, probably for different purposes.

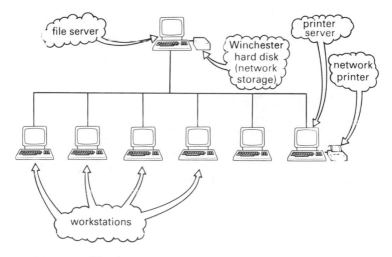

Fig. 9.13 *A small local area network*

A very simple network might consist of, say, 15 microcomputers which act as *terminals* or *workstations*. One machine is normally dedicated to the running of the system and is known as the *file server*. In a small system, the file server is responsible for the retrieval and distribution of programs and data from *backing storage*. Network backing storage is normally a *Winchester hard disk*.

A typical local area network would include:

File server: dedicated micro with Winchester hard disk, 20–100 megabytes
Tape streamer: fast cassette cartridge used for backing up (archiving)
Cabling: about 1 kilometre
Workstations: 10–100 microcomputers or dumb terminals

A further machine acts as the network *printer server* and this may only be used as a workstation when printing is not taking place across the network.

In education, the Acorn Econet system and the Research Machines Nimbus Network are popular. In business and higher education the Ethernet system is used with IBM-compatible machines.

The fact that all of a network system's data can be kept on one central disk storage device is very convenient but also dangerous. Failure of the system could lead to the loss of all of a firm's records, the whole of a school's educational software, or students' projects, representing several months' work. To prevent such a disaster it is essential to make *back-up* copies of all important files, on a regular basis. This might be done daily, with all the

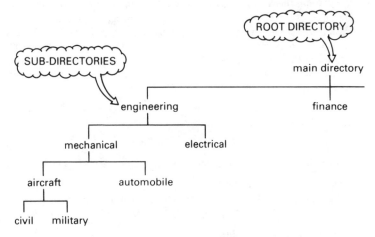

Fig. 9.14 *The hierarchical structure of network files*

day's work being copied onto a floppy disk or a tape streamer; this process is known as *archiving*. The tape streamer used on the RM Nimbus network has a cartridge capable of saving 23 megabytes of data at a transfer rate of 5 megabytes per minute.

Since there will be a large number of users, the files on the disk are organised in a sophisticated *tree system* of *directories*. As with an actual tree, everything starts from the root: the *root directory* is the main directory – all other directories are *sub-directories* from the root. A simplified example of this hierarchical structure might be as follows:

System management
Each group of users would be allocated their own area of the disk, say 200 kilobytes (1K = 1024 characters). The *system manager* has certain privileges which allow him or her to *create* and *delete users* and if necessary, increase their allocation of disk space. In order to gain access to their directory, the user must '*log-on*' with their *user name* and, if desired, a *password*. These prevent unauthorised access to files. Each individual user within a department may be granted their own *sub-directory*, within their department's *main directory*.

The creation of this hierarchical structure of directories is under the control of the system manager. The manager is also responsible for the *day-to-day running* of the system, including the making of back-up copies.

Various *levels of access* to files are possible, so that access to important or private files can be restricted to certain approved users. Typical access levels are:

- *Read/write*: the person who 'owns' the files can both read and alter the files, e.g. a student developing his or her own program for project work.
- *Read only* access: an important database may be available for all users to read but files cannot be altered. The system manager can access all files for both read and write access.
- No access: some users may not be allowed any access at all to certain files, e.g. personal/confidential records, business accounts or designs.

The system manager is able to control the levels of access to the files.

KEY FACTS
Access to important network files is restricted by:

- passwords and user identities
- different levels of access (Read Only, Read and Write, No Access)

Multi-access to the same data
A network of terminals around a central computer in a large company

allows *many users* to access the *same data*; an example is in the automobile industry where many different departments need to look at drawings of the same components. The drawing may be stored as a file in a central computer, accessed by terminals in the various departments. This gives great savings in time and efficiency compared with the previous system where drawings were only held on paper ('blueprints') in stores around a large company. When data is held centrally, modifications to a design will be immediately available to all users, so that no-one should be working with obsolete data.

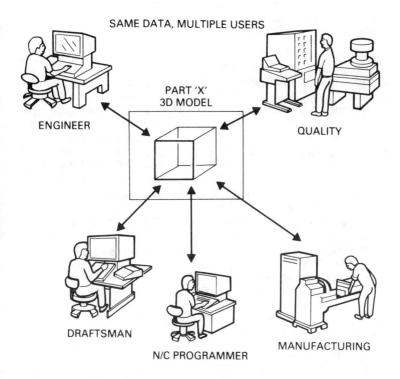

Fig. 9.15 *A multi-access system within the Ford Motor Company Ltd*

Multi-access systems are also used in the accountancy and stock control departments of large companies and in airline seat reservation. It is important that these systems operate in *real-time* so that the data is always up-to-date.

KEY FACTS

Local Area Networks (LANs) may consist of a large number of micro-computers connected to a central storage unit (file server/hard disk); **Multi-Access** systems consist of a set of terminals (either 'dumb' or 'intelligent') connected to a central mainframe or minicomputer. The advantages of LANs are:

- shared access to expensive storage and printing devices
- ability to share expensive software (programs)
- ability to share and update the same data files

Hospital diagnostics

A large amount of data must be handled by hospital staff during the diagnosis of a patient's illness; blood samples, etc. are analysed in the laboratory and the results stored together with other data concerning the patient. The *patient's records* must be *cumulative* so that a complete and up-to-date case history is available, including the results of previous tests. These records should be easily accessible so that enquiries may be made during any subsequent treatment. Hospital administrators must keep records and statistics when monitoring the *costs* and *workloads* of the various departments. Traditional systems using paper and card index systems are extremely slow, inefficient and not easily accessible to all of the hospital staff involved.

The Hospital Diagnostic Service enables patient records to be stored on a minicomputer using a Winchester hard disk backing store. The results of any laboratory tests on the patient can be input either by typing at a VDU terminal or via an '*RS232 interface*'. The RS232 interface is a device which connects the laboratory testing instruments directly to the computer. Automatic recording of data by computer in this way is known as *data logging*. Once stored on disk these records may be interrogated by medical and clerical staff in the continuing care of the patient.

Some of the advantages of this system include:

- Very large quantities of data are stored more compactly than in previous paper/card index systems.
- Searching (interrogation) of patient records is much faster and more efficient.
- Data can be input and output easily by staff without specialist computer training.
- Accurate information is available to medical, clerical and managerial staff, from convenient VDU terminals around the hospital.
- Updating to give cumulative patient records is more easily accomplished than by manual methods.

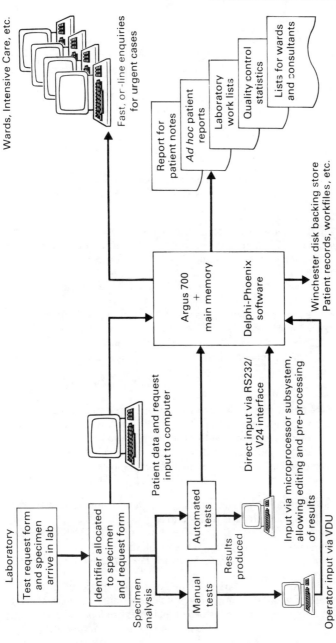

Fig. 9.16 *The Delphi-Phoenix Hospital Diagnostic Service (a network of VDU terminals based around the Ferranti Argus 700 minicomputer)*

1 A newspaper publisher uses electronic mail to communicate between its many branch offices. The system uses the telephone system and a modem.

What is the purpose of the modem?

(MEG Specimen Paper 1, Section E, Qu. 21)

2 (*a*) Explain what is meant by a viewdata service such as PRESTEL.
  (*b*) Explain what is meant by a teletext service such as CEEFAX and ORACLE.
  (*c*) What are the differences between viewdata services such as PRE-STEL and teletext services such as CEEFAX and ORACLE?

(NEA Specimen Paper 2, Qu. 4)

3 To send a letter with an electronic mail system, you would type it in on your keyboard, and it would be sent to a central computer. Each time that you connect to the computer, you will be given a list of the letters waiting for you.
  (*a*) Give *one* advantage of electronic mail compared with sending a letter by post.
  (*b*) Give *one* advantage compared with using the telephone.
  (*c*) Post Office workers are concerned over the widespread use of electronic mail. Give *one* reason for this concern.
  (*d*) Give an example of an item which could not be sent by electronic mail.

(LEAG Specimen Paper 1, Qu. 15)

4 Jobs are being affected by the increased use of electronic mail.
  (*a*) Choose a job which will be lost or adversely affected as a result of the increased use of electronic mail and explain why.
  (*b*) Choose a job which will be improved or made easier by the increased use of electronic mail and explain why.

(NEA Specimen Paper 2, Qu. 7)

5 The system whereby users and the computer communicate with each other through terminals is referred to as
A random processing **B** analogue computing **C** batch processing
D interactive computing **E** job assembling

(NISEC Specimen Paper III, Section A, Qu. 12)

6 A chain store uses a large number of on-line POS (point-of-sale) terminals. Describe the advantages of these terminals being connected to a mainframe computer instead of their being independent.

(MEG Specimen Paper 3, Section A, Qu. 11)

7   Give *two* ways of making sure that the wrong people cannot use remote
    terminals to access information held on a computer system.
                                            (LEAG Specimen Paper 1, Qu. 14)

8   Explain why a stolen cash dispenser card is of little use to a thief.
                                        (MEG Specimen Paper 2, Section D, Qu. 4)

9   Miss Gillespie needs to make an urgent change to a file which she has
    already keyed in and saved while working in the Computer Room.
    However, she finds that she cannot get into the Computer Room. 'No
    problem,' says a friend, 'Why not use the machine in the library? It is
    one of the stations on the network and can access a central file store.'
    Miss Gillespie is puzzled.
    (*a*) Explain to her what is meant by a station on the network.
    (*b*) Why does she not have to go to the Computer Room to make the
           change?
                                (SEB Standard Grade 1988 General Level, Qu. 2(d))

10 List *three* items of data which would be input to an EFTPOS system.
                                        (MEG Specimen Paper 1, Section G, Qu. 8)

11 (*a*) What is meant by a multi-access computer?
    (*b*) Why do users of multi-access computers usually have to have a
           user's password?
    (c)   Three levels of access to files held on a computer backing store are:

           read and write, read only, forbidden.

           Give an appropriate situation for each of these.
                                            (SEG Specimen Paper 2, Qu. 8)

Many people are worried or confused by computers. This is often true of those who have not experienced information technology at school. Some of the main fears which people hold (rightly or wrongly) are:

- Computers may cause unemployment.
- Computers may be damaged by pressing the wrong key.
- Computers make mistakes.
- Computers are difficult to use and may involve retraining.
- Health may be damaged by long term exposure to VDU screens – alleged injury to the unborn child.
- Private and personal information may fall into the wrong hands. Information might be used for political purposes.
- Important data may be lost by accident or theft.
- Money may be lost through computer crime.
- Computers are out-of-date as soon as they are made.

While there is some truth in many of these fears, they should be balanced by also considering the advantages which computers may bring:

- Computers are generally faster, more accurate and reliable than people.
- Computers don't need tea-breaks or get tired, so firms may become more successful and release people from boring and repetitive jobs.
- Most people find computers less tiring to use than older equipment – the wordprocessor requires less effort than the manual typewriter.
- Computers can *simulate* tests or experiments which may be expensive or dangerous in real life – for example, flight simulators.
- The electronic office or computer-controlled factory is generally cleaner and tidier than the older work environment. Data is stored more compactly on disks than on loose sheets of paper.
- Computers can work in difficult or dangerous conditions, e.g. bomb disposal robots or computer-controlled mini-submarines.

Overcoming the fears

Some of the anxieties of people may be overcome by enlightened companies. It might be helpful to:

- train all employees in computer literacy to remove the 'mystique' of computers. Explain that mistakes are normally caused by incorrect data being supplied to the computer (GIGO – Garbage In, Garbage Out). Explain that a computer is really a machine which carries out instructions programmed by people
- point out that employees whose jobs have been replaced by computer may be *retrained* to do new and more interesting work

- explain that computers are needed to help firms to be more efficient and keep prices down; this should help the firm to be more successful and hence create or at least save jobs
- ensure that all files are kept secure from unauthorised access; create systems of back-up disks and tapes to prevent accidental loss or damage of important files
- ensure that all VDU operators, etc. have regular breaks and do not spend too many hours in front of a screen
- Make sure all computer systems are thoroughly tested; employees should be given proper training before new systems are introduced
- ensure that suitable checks (validation) are built into programs to trap faulty data; this might, for instance, prevent a customer receiving a bill for £1000 say, when expecting one for £10

Jobs lost

The effect of computers on job losses is not clear in some situations; a secretary may spend less time actually typing after changing to a word-processor. The secretary is not made redundant, but the job may now involve other activities such as using a *spreadsheet* program for accounts. The use of computers in banks has reduced the number of clerks who used to complete ledgers or accounts by hand; new tasks are now undertaken, such as 'marketing' new banking services to customers.

In manufacturing industry, there has been a net loss of jobs due to the increased use of computers, for example:

- the use of robots for welding and spraying car body shells
- computer-controlled manufacture of aero-engine components
- the decline of the Swiss watch industry (clockwork mechanisms) and replacement by the Japanese digital electronic watch
- the use of computers for the electronic typesetting of newspapers – replacing the skills of many craftsmen setting newsprint by hand

Personal data and the Data Protection Act

Computers now store vast amounts of data about people; much of this data is private and other people have no right to see it. Examples of *personal* data are:

- a person's name and address
- medical and social security records
- police/criminal records
- career details/examination qualifications
- marital status and family history
- financial status – details of bank accounts, savings and salary

In order to protect the citizen against the misuse of personal data on computer files, the government introduced the Data Protection Act. Under this Act, anyone who stores data which identifies a person must register with the Data Protection Registrar. The law requires the *data user* (the person storing the data on computer) to declare the purpose of the data and to take all reasonable steps to ensure that the data is:

- secure from unauthorised access; not disclosed to other people
- accurate and up-to-date
- available for inspection by the *data subject* (the person identified by the data); the data subject may insist that inaccurate records are corrected
- not used for purposes other than that originally intended

Some typical examples of the abuse of personal data are:

- the use of health or criminal records to damage a person's reputation or job prospects
- the use of names and addresses leading to unwanted sales approaches, unsolicited mail

In the home

The advent of computer technology has impinged on many aspects of the home. *Microprocessors*, as discussed earlier, are used to control electronic devices such as washing machines, televisions and cookers. These undoubtedly help to make life easier and the home may be run more efficiently. In the future, more use may be made of microprocessors to control services such as heating and lighting.

Home computers consisting of keyboards and screens are mainly used for playing games. Other home uses include wordprocessing and computer programming. Children may use computers for educational purposes and their parents may use a computer to help with the management of a small business. The advent of cheap IBM-compatible computers such as the Amstrad PC 1512 and PC 1640 means that people may continue to work at home on disks prepared at the office. This was not possible for many people in the past when business micros costing several thousand pounds were needed to run IBM software.

In the future, increasing use of computers may be made in areas such as *home banking*, *home shopping* and *electronic videotex services* like Prestel.

The *disabled* find computers most helpful for tasks such as wordprocessing. Using only a small movement of the head, for example, they can use the computer to write complex reports or university doctoral theses.

A number of people now work from home with computers connected to headquarters by a modem and the telephone line. This pattern of working may suit a parent with young children or someone who prefers to live in the country rather than the city. The disadvantage is that some people may feel *isolated* and miss the contact with colleagues which office workers enjoy.

In education

Britain has been a leader in the field of educational computing; the BBC Micro introduced in the early 1980s has been dominant in primary and secondary education. Computers have been used in schools for:

- Computer Assisted Learning – CAL
- Computer Studies (for GCSE) and Computer Appreciation/Information Technology
- School Administration – form lists, timetables, etc.

In the future, wider use will be made across all aspects of the school curriculum. Packages such as the spreadsheet, wordprocessor and database allow *Information Technology* to be used as a *tool* in various subjects – not just the single subject Computer Studies.

Considerable argument has taken place over the need for schools and colleges to adopt the IBM standard of computer software used in businesses throughout the world. To this end, the latest educational computers, such as the Acorn Archimedes and the Research Machines RM Nimbus, are able to run IBM business software. This is done by the use of *IBM 'emulator' programs*, which enable the computer to accept the IBM-type operating system known as MSDOS. Both the Archimedes and the Nimbus are very powerful computers, enabling students to use equipment as sophisticated as that in business.

Fig. 10.1   *Acorn Archimedes*

Fig. 10.2   *RM Nimbus*

At work
People who work with computers can be divided into two main categories:

- computer users
- professional computing or data processing staff

Computer users
Many people use computers to help with their main job which may have nothing to do with computers; the computer is used as a tool to make their work easier, faster or more efficient. The computer user may have attended short courses, for example on how to use a software package such as a spreadsheet or database. Typical computer users may include, for example:

- doctors (checking patients' records)
- teachers (use in art, languages, music, etc.)
- managers (monitoring accounts or sales)
- comedians (filing jokes)
- vicars (wordprocessing sermons)
- bank staff (checking balances)
- advertising agencies (desktop publishing)
- architects (designing houses)
- pop musicians (composing and arranging)

Some computer users, for example scientists, engineers and teachers, acquire the programming skills needed to write specialist programs for their own work. Their level of programming skills may be as high as that of the professional programmer – although their first priority is not computing but the demands of their main job.

Computer professionals
New types of employment have evolved with the arrival of the Information Revolution; this may be compared with the changes occurring in the Industrial Revolution. Computer professionals have normally received specialised training to work with computers, extending over a period of several months or years.

These jobs are involved in the design, manufacture, selling, installation and maintenance of computers and their software. The manufacture of computers and their components (for example, silicon chips) tends to be concentrated in 'high-tech' science parks or industrial estates in various parts of the world. One of the most famous is Silicon Valley in California; in Britain smaller groupings of computer firms are found in Scotland and Cambridge – sometimes jokingly referred to as Silicon 'Glen' and Silicon 'Fen' respectively.

The new high-tech industries – 'start-up' companies – are also helping to reduce unemployment in areas where traditional industries are in decline;

for example, coal mining in South Wales and steel making in Durham.

In large companies the specialised computing staff are often organised into a separate department – *Data Processing*.

Data processing staff
The DP staff are normally organised in a 'hierarchical' structure, branching down from the top – the *data processing manager*.

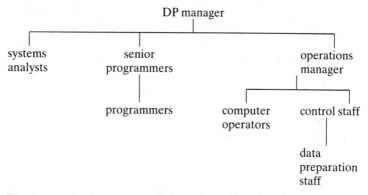

The data processing manager is normally responsible for the appointment of new staff; the evaluation of new hardware (computers) and recommendations for purchase; planning the workload of the department to serve the needs of the whole company within a budget set by the top management of the company.

The operations manager must supervise the operations staff such as *computer operators* and *data preparation staff*. This will include controlling overtime and shiftworking and allocating tasks to employees. The operations manager may also order new consumable supplies such as printer paper and ribbons.

The computer operator controls the computer via a simplified keyboard known as a *console*. The job involves loading new programs and data files from disk or tape, refilling the printer with paper, and taking appropriate action when errors occur. Computer operators normally work shifts on large computer systems; this ensures that expensive equipment is kept running all day and all night.

Data preparation staff usually key-in vast quantities of data while sitting at VDU terminals – normally using the *key-to-disk* system. The job is similar to typing and also involves *verification*; this means typing all data a second time for checking purposes. Much argument has taken place over alleged health problems from VDU screens, but medical opinion is divided; some doctors would say that the radiation emitted is infinitesimally small and much less than that encountered in many aspects of normal life. However, there is no doubt that the VDU operator needs good eyesight and frequent breaks from working, to prevent eyestrain.

Control staff monitor the delivery of new jobs to the data processing department. Accurate records are kept so that completed output is returned to the correct department. Large companies also record the amount of *Central Processing Time* (CPU time) on each job and charge the various departments accordingly.

Where vast amounts of data are kept on magnetic tape, these must be stored in large racks, forming *tape libraries*. The control of the storage and issuing of magnetic tapes and disks is carried out by the **file librarian**.

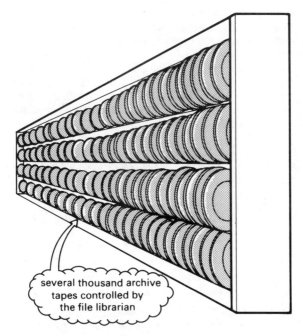

several thousand archive tapes controlled by the file librarian

Fig. 10.3 *Part of a magnetic tape library*

Programmers Apart from writing new programs, the programmer may work on the modification and improvement of existing programs – *program maintenance*. The programmer may also write the documentation or instruction manuals for both computer users and also other programmers needing to work on the program. (*User documentation* and *program documentation*, respectively.) Program documentation would be needed when a programmer leaves the team and their work is continued by someone else.

Programmers in large companies work in teams, so that each programmer is responsible for a small part or *module* of the main program.

Applications programmers work in high level languages such as COBOL, FORTRAN, Pascal or C and write *application packages*, e.g. for handling a payroll system.

Systems programmers work in machine code or assembly language and write the programs needed to control the computer itself; these might include a *language compiler* or a *disk operating system*.

The systems analysts are normally former programmers; their main job is to advise on the suitability of using computers for certain tasks. For example, a large company might consider using computers to take care of all travel arrangements – booking flights and hotels and keeping a record of all expense accounts. The systems analyst would carry out a thorough investigation of the existing *manual system*. The costs and time taken using the traditional manual methods would be compared with the costs and time saved in the computer system. This investigation to see if the use of computers is worthwhile is known as a *feasibility study*.

The result of the feasibility study will usually be a report to the management of the organisation; this will summarise both the benefits and costs of introducing a computer system. The management may decide that the use of computers will provide a faster, cheaper and more efficient service;

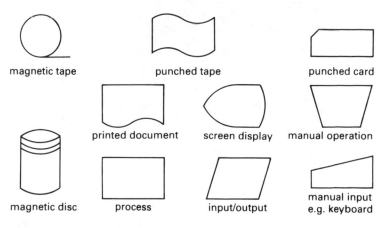

Fig. 10.4 *Symbols used in systems flowcharts*

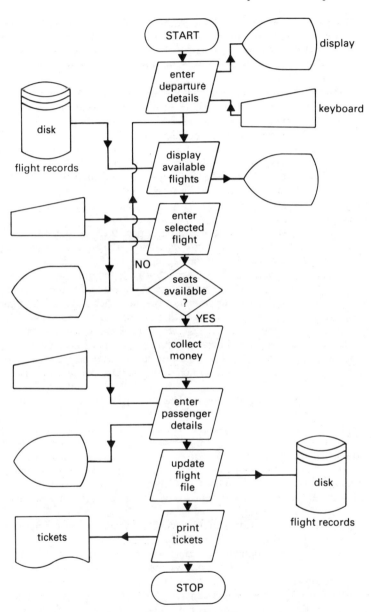

Fig. 10.5 *Systems flowchart – airline booking system*

alternatively, it may decide that the old-fashioned manual system is still the best. There may also be other factors to consider: will the staff be prepared to retrain? Will there be redundancies and will the unions accept them? These factors were important issues in the introduction of computers to the newspaper industry.

If it is decided to computerise, the systems analyst will draw up a *systems flowchart* outlining the flow of data through the various stages of the process. The systems flowchart also specifies the various *media* used, such as magnetic disks, tapes and paper documents.

The systems analyst will recommend suitable equipment (hardware and software). If necessary, new software will be written by programmers within the company (*in-house* programmers); or software will be commissioned from a company specialising in writing computer programs – a *software house*. The systems analyst will also design all the necessary forms and data capture sheets.

Once the programs have been written, a period of thorough *testing* is required using carefully selected *test data* to find all the errors or 'bugs' – this is the *debugging* phase. Then the new computer system must be gradually introduced – the *implementation* phase. Normally the old manual system and the new computer system are kept running side-by-side until everyone has complete confidence in the computer system. A period of staff training will certainly be necessary. Keeping both the manual and computer systems in operation together is known as *parallel running*. If calculations are involved, the computer results will be checked by manual calculations using pencil and paper. This is known as a *dry run*. It is not always necessary to write new software from scratch. For many applications, existing spreadsheet and database programs are available 'off-the-shelf'; for example dBASE III is a very powerful database package suitable for many applications.

After the new computer system has been implemented and is in regular use, a period of careful watching or *monitoring* is necessary. This is to ensure that the system is performing as expected and achieving the predicted savings in time and costs. Each year a thorough *review* will be made and, if necessary, decisions taken to modify and improve the system.

The responsibilities of the systems analyst may be summarised as follows:

- *Feasibility study* – finding out if a computer system will be an improvement on the existing manual system.
- *System design* – producing system flowcharts, methods of data capture, etc., based on a study of the old system; specifying suitable hardware and software.
- *Programming* – the systems analyst will supervise the programmers 'coding' the various operations and calculations in a high level language such as COBOL, Pascal, FORTRAN or C.

- *Implementation* – setting up the new system, including testing with suitable data; staff training. Parallel running of both old and new systems.
- *Monitoring* and *post-implementation review* – longer term close scrutiny of the new computer system to check and improve on the performance of the system.

Computer bureaux

Some smaller companies may not have the capital or the staff necessary to set up a computer system. In this case the firm may send its data to a computer bureau – a computer firm which takes in other companies' work. Some large companies use their spare computer time to offer bureau services to other firms, for example by offering a complete payroll service. Or access to the computer may be given via terminals in a *time-sharing* agreement.

1   It has been suggested that the increasing use of computer systems will produce a society where most people are unemployed. Do you think this is true? Give *two* reasons to support your answer.

(SEG Specimen Paper 2, Qu. 9(b))

2   A health centre has stored the personal details of local patients in a computer system. Give *two* items of data which the system would hold and why they would be needed.

(NEA Specimen Paper 2, Qu. 5(a))

3   Choose *two* applications from the given list to complete the sentence.

          social security payments   medical records
          aircraft flight simulation   weather forecasting
Personal data is used when a computer keeps files of information for
. . . . or . . . .

(MEG Specimen Paper 1, Section G, Qu. 7)

4   When microcomputers are used to automate work, some human jobs disappear, some change, and some are new. If office work is automated suggest, with a reason for each:
   (*a*) one human job which will disappear,
   (*b*) one human job which will change,
   (*c*) one new one which will appear.

(SEG Specimen Paper 2, Qu. 9(a))

5   Describe health hazards which can arise when a person uses a visual display unit for a long period of time.

(NEA Specimen Paper 2, Qu. 1(b))

6   A firm that has not used a computer before has ordered one for delivery in a year's time. State *three* things which the firm should do to prepare for the arrival of the computer.

(LEAG Specimen Paper 3, Qu. 8)

7   A firm installs a computer system to work out the wages. How could they test that it is working properly?

(LEAG Specimen Paper 1, Qu. 7)

8   Give *three* tasks that a systems analyst normally does.

(SEG Specimen Paper 2, Qu. 6)

9   When a new computer system is installed it is normal for parallel running to take place. What is meant by parallel running?

(LEAG Specimen Paper 3, Qu. 6)

10   Computers started to appear only around forty years ago. Prior to that,

people managed to live and progress without them. List *four* reasons why a society such as ours finds computers useful.

(SEB Ordinary Grade 1988, Section 1, Qu. 2)

11 By completing the diagram below show how the staff of a Data Processing Department might be organised. Include *four* different personnel in your diagram.

Data Processing Manager

(WJEC Specimen Paper 1, Qu. 12)

12 A Computer Department employs computer operators, systems analysts, a file librarian and keyboard operators.

Who would do the following tasks?

(*a*) Carry out a feasibility study.

(*b*) Act on messages from the operating system.

(*c*) Copy from source documents.

(*d*) Maintain an index of files.

(*e*) Load paper into a printer.

(*f*) Operate a key-to-disk system.

(*g*) Verify data.

(*h*) Design source documents.

(MEG 1987 Paper 2 Section D, Qu. 10)

APPENDIX
Project work for GCSE Computer Studies

Apart from the written examination for GCSE Computer Studies, you *must* produce one or more *coursework projects*. These contribute about a quarter to one third of the total marks for the course. The project is assessed by marking a written report which you write throughout the two years of the course. There is no practical examination in Computer Studies; all evidence of your work with the computer must be contained in your project report or *documentation*.

Your teacher will give details of the sort of projects which you may attempt but two points should be borne in mind when choosing a subject:

- The project should solve a *realistic* and sensible problem – it must really need the use of computers and should not be trivial.
- The work should be your own; any material which is 'borrowed' must be clearly identified as such. You must not, for example, copy programs out of books or magazines and then claim them as your own original work.

The type of project to be undertaken could take any of three forms:

Category A   Writing an original computer program or suite of programs.
Category B   Developing an existing program by adding your own improvements and extensions.
Category C   Using an existing package (which someone else has written) to solve a problem. This includes spreadsheets, databases, etc.

As mentioned earlier, your complete set of coursework may comprise more than one project; so you might complete, say, two projects from two different categories.

Whatever you decide to do for project work, it must cover certain important topics or skills for GCSE. Check with your teacher that your subject covers these requirements; you might need to do two quite different projects which complement each other in order to cover the wide range of computing skills needed.

Categories A and B – writing or developing a program
This is a very popular topic for projects but is not necessarily the easiest. Programs need to be written in a clear and structured style – a program written as a jumbled mass of 'spaghetti' will not earn many marks if it cannot be read easily. The program should be divided into a set of clearly defined *modules* or *procedures*, whose purpose is obvious. The use of the GOTO statement should be avoided at all times.

The *top-down* method should be used; plan out the *broad outline* of the various sections of the program – perhaps drawing a flowchart. Converting to programming code in a language like BASIC, COMAL or Logo is done *after* all the planning is complete.

If developing a program for a project, the following should be borne in mind:

- Make *printouts* on paper (of both *listings* and *output*) at regular intervals.
- Label the printouts with the date and notes of any changes.

Try to write up the history of the development of your program as the work proceeds, from the start. This is much easier than attempting to write the report after all the computer work is finished (when many other people are trying to use the same printer).

If your program is a development of one written by someone else, try to maintain the *style* of the original program. This means that if, say, the program consists of procedures or sub-routines driven from a menu, any new work is done by extending the menu and adding new procedures.

Possible programming (or program extension) projects might be:

- a *database* program on any subject of your choice – animal records, vehicles, personal details, parish records. Ask your teachers for any card index systems which might be computerised.
- an *educational* program, for example for revision in physics, geography, languages, etc.
- a program to do *calculations* in science or mathematics.
- a *graphics* design, for example a house, a map, a piece of machinery such as a cycle or a company logo.

Category C – using an existing package

Many packages are available in schools and colleges, the main ones being wordprocessors, spreadsheets, databases, communications (electronic mail), art/design and desktop publishing. Care must be taken to choose a package which covers a substantial number of the GCSE skills or criteria needed. It is unlikely that a wordprocessing package on its own will cover many of the skills; however, a joint spreadsheet and wordprocessing project may be very successful.

Many tasks around your school or college are suitable for computerisation with a spreadsheet, wordprocessor or database. Ask your teachers for examples of mark lists, form lists or worksheets which could be improved by using a computer.

Of course, whatever the category of project, its appearance might be improved by producing the *documentation* itself on a *wordprocessor*.

Essential points

All projects should include:

- samples of all planning and preparation sheets on paper (for example, designs of records, computer graphics produced by hand)
- a clear description of the input required and the expected output
- proof of successful computer running – either printed output (hard copy), screen dumps or photographs of the screen. Programming projects should include complete program listings – *annotated*, i.e. described, to explain what each section does
- description of the various stages of the development of the project, including the way problems have been solved
- discussion of the merits of different methods used – for example, would a *mouse* be more suitable for input than the *keyboard*?
- descriptions of any checks or *validation*, to prevent unsuitable data from being entered
- conclusions: compare the program or package with any previous manual methods – what are the advantages or disadvantages of using the computer?
- suggestions for further work. What could be done if more time or better hardware and software were available?

The overall presentation will be improved if the project is enclosed in a clear plastic folder with a title page, contents page and bibliography.

Further guidance and suggestions for project work for GCSE Computer Studies can be obtained from two books by the same author:

Software Activities for GCSE
Programming Activities for GCSE

both published by Edward Arnold/Hodder & Stoughton.

ANSWERS TO QUESTIONS

The following answers are the sole responsibility of the author and have not been provided by the examination boards. For many questions there are alternative answers in addition to those provided in this section. The Midland Examining Group does not permit the use of model answers and so for some questions no answers are provided in this section. In this case the reader should refer to the relevant chapter in the text; it is also possible to obtain complete specimen papers from the examining boards. These include model answers. (Please refer to the list of addresses in the front of this book.)

1 Computer systems

1 Micro: secretary
   Mini: college
   Mainframe: Local Authority

2 Control Unit
   Arithmetic and Logic Unit (ALU)
   Immediate Access Store (Memory)

3 Magnetic tape and disk
   The contents of memory (programs and data) are lost when the computer is switched off.

4 terminal

5 A

6 RAM can be 'written' to and read from, ROM is read only. ROM cannot be changed.

7 Use only the binary digits 0 and 1.

8 Printer interface

9 On a train for wordprocessing.

10 See text.

11 (a) A byte is 8 bits
   (b) Store locations 1 or more bytes wide each with a separate address. Each character is 1 byte.

12 (1) character (2) instruction (3) address

13 (a) Disk drive (b) Database program

14 (a) Language compiler (b) Accounts program

15 peripheral units

16 B

2   The input phase
1   Keyboard, mouse, joystick, lightpen, bar code reader, digitiser

2   Easier to draw freely

3   See text

4   (*a*) Bank cheques: machine readable, fast, secure
  (*b*) Bills readable by humans and machine
  (*c*) Readers are expensive

5   See text

6   **D**

7 and **8**   See text

9   **B**

10, 11, 12   See text

3   The output phase
1   Printer, VDU (screen), graphics plotter, robot

2   (*a*) Dot-matrix, fast
  (*b*) Daisywheel, high quality letters

3   (*a*) matrix (*b*) line printer (*c*) matrix (*d*) daisywheel

4   **D**

5   (*a*) VDU (*b*) microfilm camera (*c*) line printer

6   Faster, cheaper; electricity bills

7   (*a*) Easier to read (by humans)
  (*b*) Large quantities, compact storage
  (*c*) Wordprocessing, text readable with naked eye
  (*d*) Bank statements; large number of records in a small space

8   Modifying an engineering drawing. Digitiser enables changes to be made easily; graph plotter draws lines fast and accurately.

4   Backing storage
1   (*a*) Floppy disk, hard disk
  (*b*) Disk pack, tape reel

2   (*a*) Hard disk – high storage capacity needed
  (*b*) Back-up to floppy or tape streamer

3   (*a*) Cheap (*b*) Fast retrieval

4 Permanent copy of programs and data. Exchange of data between people.

5 See text

6 **D**

7 (*a*) Systems programs, operating systems, languages
   (*b*) User's programs and data
   (*c*) RAM is needed for entering new programs and data; ROM gives fast access to systems software

8 Faster access to program (no loading)

9 Floppy disk, magnetic drum

10 See text

11 (*a*) Capacity of the tape exceeds the memory
   (*b*) Allows the tape to stop and start

12 See text

5 Representing data and instructions

1 **C**

2 **A**

3 **D**

4 31

5 See text

6 **B**

7 (*a*) 0 1 1 0 1 1
   (*b*) 1 0 0 1 0 1

8 **D**

9 (*a*) All characters have an odd number of 1s.
   (*b*) Check whether a character has been transmitted correctly.

10 (*a*) Operation code and an address. (*b*) 5A (*c*) Quicker and easier to read.

6 Central processing

1 Control Unit, Arithmetic and Logic Unit, Immediate Access Store (Memory)

2 (*a*) A register has a special purpose.
   (*b*) Holds the address of next instruction to be fetched.

(*c*) Holds the current instruction.

3 An instruction is fetched from memory and placed in the instruction register. The program counter is incremented.

4 (*a*) Supervises the execution of the program.
(*b*) Performs arithmetical operations, e.g. addition.
(*c*) Holds the current program and data.

5 Control Unit, Arithmetic and Logic Unit.

6 See text

7

Inputs				Output
R	W	T	M	P
0	0	1	0	0
0	0	1	1	0
0	1	0	0	0
0	1	0	1	1
0	1	1	0	1
0	1	1	1	1
1	0	1	1	0
1	1	0	0	0
1	1	1	0	0
1	1	1	1	0

8 See text

7 Levels of communication

1 See text

2 (*a*) Easier for humans to understand
(*b*) Programs work faster

3 Languages designed to suit different purposes: data files, science, control, AI, education

4 A program to carry out stock control

5 **D**

6 Format a new disk. Carry out sorting. Wordprocessor – to send out letters

7 See text

8 (*a*) Programs
(*b*) Translate programs into machine code

    (*c*) Interpreter translates an instruction every time it is run, compiler produces a complete program in machine code

    (*d*) Assembler translates assembly language not high level language

9 C

10 See text

8 Files and data processing

1 See text

2 (*a*) record (*b*) field

3 See text

4 Serial access: all previous records are read before the required record. Direct access: no previous records are read before the required record.

5 See text

6 A

7 See text

8 A

9 Password system

10 (*a*) A collection of organised records
    (*b*) Back-up to tape or disk

11 (*a*) New pupil joins the school.
    (*b*) A parent remarries.
    (*c*) A pupil leaves the school.
    (*d*) Make regular back-up copies on a second disk or tape.

12 Password system; only allow certain people to use the computer

13 A

14 (*a*) Verification: checking that data has been copied exactly.
       Validation: checking that data is sensible within certain limits
    (*b*) Verification: involves retyping and correcting the data – doesn't need a special program as with validation
    (*c*) Divide by 11 and take remainder as check digit
       The error may mean that an illegal or incorrect transaction has been attempted

15 (*a*) Retyping the data
    (*b*) Merging is easier if both files are in the same order – the account numbers are compared and the record with the lowest account number is written to the new file on tape
    (*c*) If the new file is lost or damaged another one can be reconstructed

9   Communications networks

1 See text

2 (*a*) A service accessed by a microcomputer and modem giving access to databases and allowing electronic communications
    (*b*) Teletext allows data to be received by television set
    (*c*) Viewdata permits sending and receiving of data, teletext only allows receiving

3 (*a*) Faster
    (*b*) No need to make personal contact
    (*c*) Jobs may be lost
    (*d*) A certificate or contract requiring an original signature

4 (*a*) Postman – fewer letters
    (*b*) Secretary – less need for envelopes, stamps, etc

5 **D**

6 See text

7 Password, encoding the data

8 See text

9 (*a*) A machine connected to the network file store by cabling for loading and saving files, printing
    (*b*) File can be loaded into the machine in the library, changed, then resaved on file store

10 See text

11 (*a*) Many people can access the CPU to run programs via terminals
    (*b*) Prevent unauthorised reading or damage to files
    (*c*) read and write: student working on a project
    read only: library programs
    forbidden: personal, health files

10   Computers and people

1 See text

2 Name: searching for records
Drugs taken: monitor side effects

3 See text

4 (*a*) ledger clerk
    (*b*) typist
    (*c*) programmer

5 Eyestrain, headache

6 Talk to the staff.
Prepare a secure room.
Employ a systems analyst to plan the system, select software

7 Calculate the wages by hand and compare

8 Analyse old systems.
Design new system – stationery, hardware, software.
Supervise changeover, implementation

9 Keeping old system going till computer system has been proved satisfactory

10 Less paperwork; faster access to more data; elimination of boring jobs; complex processes controlled, simulated

11 and **12**   See text